# CRIME AND CORRECTIONS:
# AN AL-ISLAMIC PERSPECTIVE
## by
# SIDNEY RAHIM SHARIF

Kazi Publications, Inc.
1215 W. Belmont Ave.
Chicago, IL 60657

Printed in U.S.A.

ISBN 0-935782-13-5  Paperback
ISBN 0-935782-15-X  Hardcover

# ABOUT THE AUTHOR

Sidney Rahim Sharif has been involved in the Criminal Justice System for over twenty years. As a member of the Chicago Police Department for over twenty-three years, he is longtime observer of the Criminal Justice System, especially at the usual point of entry for the common man. He has manned patrol cars, done foot patrol, and carried out squadrol assignments as well as worked with intelligence gathering and in-depth criminal investigations covering primarily violent crimes.

Mr. Sharif's commitment to reform of the Criminal Justice System goes beyond his job. He is involved in the well-respected Prison Services Program of the American Muslim Mission. He has lectured and counseled inmates at the Cook County Jail and the Federal Metropolitan Correctional Center, both in Chicago, Illinois. It is through this program that Mr. Sharif has seen results that convince him that the reforms proposed in this book are necessary and workable.

Sidney Rahim Sharif holds a B.A. Degree in the Administration of Criminal Justice from the University of Illinois-Chicago Circle. He has also earned a M.S. Degree in Corrections from Chicago State University.

# Masjid Honorable Elijah Muhammad

7351 South Stony Island Avenue    Chicago, Illinois 60649

312/667-7200,

WITH THE NAME ALLAH, MOST GRACIOUS, MOST COMPASSIONATE

MARCH 12, 1981

BROTHER SIDNEY RAHIM SHARIF
11317 SOUTH UNION
CHICAGO, ILLINOIS 60628

DEAR SIDNEY:

    YOUR BOOK 'CRIME AND CORRECTIONS' IS APPRECIATED FOR ITS
COURAGE IN EXPOSING THE HYPOCRISY ON THE PART OF AMERICA'S
LEGAL SYSTEM.  IN THAT YOUR BOOK IS NOT MERELY A BITTER CRITICISM
BUT ALSO A CREDITABLE PROPOSAL WHICH ATTEMPTS A CORRECTION,  I
ENDORSE YOUR BOLD EFFORT AND CONGRATULATE YOU AND YOUR MEMBERSHIP
IN AMERICAN MUSLIM MISSION.

    AS-SALAAM-ALAIKUM.

YOUR BROTHER IN AL'ISLAM,

*Warith Deen Muhammad*
WARITH DEEN MUHAMMAD
IMAM
AMERICAN MUSLIM MISSION

P.S.  PLEASE GIVE A COPY OF THIS MANUSCRIPT TO ME FOR MY PRIVATE
OFFICE

WDM/JR

# Table of Contents

# BISMILLAH

# WITH THE NAME ALLAH (GOD)
# THE COMPASSIONATE, THE MERCIFUL

# FOREWORD

The expressed purpose of this book is to show clearly that the leader of the American Muslim Mission, Imam Warith Deen Muhammad, has been blessed with answers and solutions to the many problems that the Criminal Justice System is presently facing. It is an effort to show that America has an alternative to her present methods of preventing crime and protecting its citizens and their properties. Imam Muhammad is freely giving his knowledge to all that have an eye to see and an ear to hear.

Any legitimate and honest authority presently working within the Criminal Justice System in America will readily admit that it is on the verge of collapse. That is to say that America has run out of lead time. The plans that are being implemented in the Criminal Justice System today should have been implemented years ago. Criminals are being produced today in such abundance that they have literally overwhelmed the system.

Imam Muhammad pointed out just a few short years ago that there is no law against practicing crime in America. The criminal laws in America are activated only if one is caught. Consequently, our Criminal Justice System is attempting to serve a society that is based on a "free for all" survival of the fittest ideology. This condition can never be reconciled; therefore, it has to be terminated.

The Bilalian (African-American) people are suffering more than any other people in America due to their own ignorance and the inadequacies of our Criminal Justice System. For example, of the 1.8 million persons under 18 who were arrested in cities in 1977, 24.6 percent were Bilalians. The greatest percentage of the victims of crimes are the Bilalian people. Young Bilalians accounted for 53.4 percent of those arrested for violent crimes and 29.7 percent of those arrested for property crimes in 1977.

In 1977, more Bilalians died at the hands of other Bilalians than all of the Bilalians killed on the battlefield during the nine-year war in Vietnam. This war only caused 614 Bilalian deaths per year. Even though we represent a minority, the Bilalian is more likely to

i

be victimized than any other group in America, and he is more likely to be arrested and subsequently confined in a penitentiary than any other group. This book specifically highlights some of the problems of the Bilalian (the African American) but it also addresses the basic problems that are generally found within our criminal justice system in America.

The primary concepts utilized in this presentation are those drawn from the religion of Al-Islam as taught by Imam Muhammad. Therefore, the reader should be aware of the fact that the proposed solutions are not guesswork. This work details, in clear language, how the enemy of man (the Jahcubite conspirators) has designed the Correctional System to fail. The Jahcubite simply represents a wicked mind that has conspired with similar thinkers to keep the world of humanity enslaved through ignorance.

This book proposes that the same application of divine guidance that Prophet Muhammad (peace be upon him) used 1,400 years ago, be utilized today. Al-Islam is the religion that will make us victorious in our struggle to correct the Criminal Justice System in America.

This book also asks that the reader focus his attention on the American Muslim Mission. This community, through the guidance of Allah, has made the kind of revolutionary changes that the Correctional System must make in order to continue its existence. The administrators of the Criminal Justice System will find, upon reading this book, that they can no longer continue to be influenced by corrupt Jewish (Zionist) interests. The term Jewish Zionist is defined in a later part of the book. While we certainly are not condemning all Jewish people, we must identify the historical source that generated the problems that we are facing in the criminal justice system today.

The writer proposes that the Correctional System can solve its problems, but it must be willing to take on even greater problems and, above all, it must place complete faith and trust in Allah. In the Holy Quran, Allah (God) tells us what we should do and how it should be done.

> "Let there arise out of you a band of people inviting to all that is good, enjoining what is right, and forbidding what is wrong: They are the ones to attain felicity." . . . The Holy Quran, A. Yusuf Ali translation, Surah 3:104.

The American Muslim Mission, under the leadership of Imam Warith Deen Muhammad, is that "band of people", and this community simply wants the world to study it and be rightly guided. The cost of crime in America is presently unbearable. It cannot continue.

# GLOSSARY

1. **ALLAH**

This is an Arabic word that has but one single meaning and that is, the God of all the worlds, The Creator of everything, The Inheritor, The Ruler, The King, The Most High, etc.

2. **AL-ISLAM**

The complete submission or surrender to the will of Allah. The way of life accepted by the Muslim.

3. **AMERICAN MUSLIM MISSION**

Formerly The World Community of Al-Islam in the West, formerly the Nation of Islam.

4. **AL-QURAN**

The Holy Book or Bible of the Muslims. This Book is the revelation from Allah to Prophet Muhammad. It was revealed to him in Arabia 1,400 years ago. The challenge of Allah still stands with reference to this Book. All of mankind collectively cannot duplicate one (Ayat) verse like it.

5. **BILALIAN**

The name chosen by members of the American Muslim Mission that properly identifies the African-American as an ethnic group of people from African and Islamic descent. Bilal was an outstanding historical figure in the history of Al-Islam. He was an Ethiopian slave prior to his accepting Al-Islam. Bilal was the first Muezzin or caller to prayer during the life of Prophet Muhammad. He was chosen by the Prophet because of his sincerity, his courage, and devotion.

6. **DEVIL**

A wicked mind that will not submit, willingly, to the will of God and seeks to corrupt mankind with the intentions of leading man away from the guidance of God.

7. **HADITH**

Authentic statements, verified by the Companions of Prophet Muhammad that address social problems and other issues that were made by Prophet Muhammad.

8. **IMAM WARITH DEEN MUHAMMAD** — The leader of the largest, identifiable, Muslim community in America. Imam means, literally, "one who is out front", a leader of prayer, one who sets the standards. Warith means inheritor. Faith is given through inheritance.

9. **JAHCUBITE** — This is a term coined by Imam Warith Deen Muhammad. This describes one who conspires with others like himself to dominate the world's people through lies, trickery and deceit. He does so with the feeling that he is doing God a favor.

10. **MUSLIM** — Anyone or anything that submits to the will of Allah, willingly or unwillingly. Everything in creation submits to the will of Allah; therefore, everything and everyone is Muslim by nature.

11. **PROPHET MUHAMMAD IBN ABDULLAH** — The last Messenger of God. Prophet Muhammad (Peace be upon him) was born in Arabia 1,400 years ago, about 571 A.D. He was Allah's blessing to mankind as the only Universal Prophet with the revelation that reconciled with the teachings of all the Prophets prior to his time.

12. **SATAN** — Devil and the term Satan are used interchangeably to describe the enemy of man. The weak mind that promises man many things, but, in reality, he promises death to man as a human being.

13. **SUNNAH** — The teachings of Prophet Muhammad. His living example and practices that Muslims follow as diligently as they follow The Quran. But, The Quran takes precedence over the Sunnah if there is a problem to be solved.

14. **ZIONISM** — A corrupt form of Jewish worship that places materialism and power over the rights of human beings.

# CHAPTER 1

## THE PRICE OF CRIME IN AMERICA

Crime touches the life of every individual in America both socially and economically. It costs untold sums of money, which comes directly or indirectly from the American workers' pockets. Through property loss, loss of productivity due to injuries, and added taxes to support the Criminal Justice System, every citizen is being drained of a large portion of his much-needed income.

Economic costs should not be the only factor that shape our attitudes towards crime. Economics should not be the only concern (that is, loss of revenue), because some can argue that they are legitimately earning more money because of the increased criminal behavior in our society. The Criminal Justice System consists of very large bureaucracies within our local, state, and federal governments. These bureaucracies consume huge amounts of revenue annually and they all are inclined to struggle against each other to increase their powers through greater numbers and areas of responsibility.

Therefore, we must concern ourselves with the other factors that are just as significant, if not more so, in shaping our attitudes towards crime in America. There are costs in lost or damaged lives, the cost of fear in the home and the community, the cost of suffering, and the cost of stress due to the failure to control one's life. These costs can be far more damaging than any monetary losses. The aforementioned losses cannot be calculated in terms of dollars and cents. But, if this were possible, we would no longer be willing to bear it, because this cost would clearly demonstrate how rapidly our society is declining. For example, crime is destroying generations of Bilalians (African-American people). The 1977 statistics from the F.B.I. Uniform Crime Reports (UCR) indicated that there were 1,639 Bilalian murder victims between the ages of 15 and 19. In 1976, 131 of every 1,000 Bilalian households were burglarized as compared with 84 of every 1,000 Caucasian households, and 14 of every 1,000 Bilalians were robbed as compared with 6 of every 1,000 Caucasians. We will deal more specifically with the aforementioned losses in other parts of this book.

Presently, we will concern ourselves with the monetary loss due to the nature of crime. There are many elements within the nature of crime that impose a heavy economic burden upon the community. Crime will determine the number of policemen a city will or should have. It will determine the size of a plant's security force, or the amount of insurance any individual or business carries. The cost of goods and services made available to the consumer is automatically inflated because of the necessary security precautions.

Crimes are being perpetrated in America every day and at any given time. Crimes may range from vagrancy and prostitution to narcotic sales and murder. America is shaken morally by epidemics of child abuse, suicides, corruption in government, and costly petty thefts. Crime in America has no bounds relative to class or ethnicity. Upon close observation, it would be accurate to say that crime in our society is a fixed way of life. For example, many leading criminologists are in support of a move to eliminate so-called "victimless" crimes from the criminal law categories. These are crimes of gambling, alcoholism, and sex related crimes such as prostitution, adultery, etc. This attitude encourages crime. It has also been proposed, on numerous occasions, that the use of drugs be removed from the realm of criminal law. In other words, these crimes are not crimes. Is this logic?

The monetary cost of crime can never be accurately calculated when a Federal, State or Local official receives a gift that influences his legislative vote. This is a costly and very serious offense regardless of how it may be viewed. When funds of the taxpayers are misappropriated, or when a company uses a man's labor without just compensation, it costs the citizen and the country money. Insurance companies are constantly increasing their rates to customers because of alleged fraudulent claims. For example, arson is a crime that kills and destroys; yet, it is used consistently to defraud insurance companies. In 1974, there was an estimated $1.3 billion loss due to arson. Many Bilalian communities are not insured properly due to higher insurance rates because of the frequent incidence of arson in most of our major cities. Arson-for-profit has rapidly become an American way of life.

In 1965, President Lyndon Johnson established the Commission on Law Enforcement and Administration of Justice. This Commission produced a reference book entitled: **Challenge of Crime in a Free Society.** This Commission was established through Executive Order No. 11236 with the following instructions: Inquire into the causes of crime and delinquency, and/or improving law enforcement and the administration of criminal justice. It is from this report and others that we obtained some of the financial and social data relative to crime.

The following chart is the "Crime Clock" of 1978 which was composed by the Federal Bureau of Investigation through its UCR. This crime clock vividly demonstrates how we all are affected every second, minute and hour by crime.

2

# CRIME CLOCK 1978

one
MURDER
every 27 minutes

one
FORCIBLE
RAPE
every 8 minutes

one
VIOLENT
CRIME
every 30 seconds

one
ROBBERY
every 76 seconds

one
CRIME INDEX
OFFENSE
every 3 seconds

one
AGGRAVATED
ASSAULT
every 57 seconds

one
BURGLARY
every 10 seconds

one
PROPERTY
CRIME
every 3 seconds

one
LARCENY-
THEFT
every 5 seconds

one
MOTOR
VEHICLE
THEFT
every 32 seconds

In 1965, $2.2 billion was spent by the local police departments in America in their efforts to combat and control crime. In 1975, we spent a total of $10.449 billion for this same effort, an increase of five times the cost within a ten-year period. In 1977, the local governments spent a total of $12.983 billion for law enforcement. These statistics indicate that the cost of local law enforcement is increasing at a rate of over 11 percent per year. This data is available through the U.S. Department of Justice, Law Enforcement Assistance Administration.

The U.S. citizens also had to pay local court expenditures during this same period at a cost of $173 million. Our State courts cost us $51 million and our Federal courts an additional $37 million. Now, of course, we had to pay to prosecute these cases along with defense costs for the indigents; this costs an additional $125 million. During any year, America's total court expenses, including prosecutions and defense, will cost its taxpayers $1.5 billion.

It should be apparent by now that it is social suicide to allow crime to continue at this rate, and we have not yet added our correctional costs. The correctional institutions, which include all Federal, State, and Local prisons, detention homes, parole and probation departments, cost the taxpayers another $5.1 billion. By doing some simple addition, we find that we have spent over $16 billion. This is not the total cost by any means. There are many other costs that cannot be calculated. But, as of 1980, it is safe to say that America's known crime control bill is over $39 billion annually.

There are other public expenditures that are directly and indirectly geared toward the prevention and control of crime. There are programs that are educational, recreational, vocational and anti-poverty that are funded primarily with State, Federal and Local government monies. These expenditures, though not included in the direct cost of combating and controlling crime, do aid in the prevention of some criminal acts, and must be considered.

The next financial cost, which is far greater than the above expenditures, is the amount lost to the public. This is the loss by the citizenry through direct offenses such as crimes against persons. These are homicides, which bring about losses of over $3.5 billion, and assaults that cost the collective taxpayers $300 million. There is another classification of crimes that are referred to as index crimes by the F.B.I. Uniform Crime Reports. These are robberies, burglaries, and larcenies which present an expense overhead of over $3.25 billion per year. Other index crimes of automobile thefts, fraud, embezzlement, forgery, property destroyed by arson and vandalism cost a sum of $19.66 billion.

4

There is another cost classification of crimes that must be added to a now inflated budget. This class of crime is referred to as illegal goods and services such as narcotics, loan sharking, prostitution, alcohol, and gambling. For these desires, the American public must pay over $11.75 billion per year. Other crimes such as driving under the influence of alcohol and tax fraud amount to approximately $9.58 billion that is lost by the public.

There are additional private costs related to crime that must be considered and added to the "crime bill". These are prevention services (alarm devices, security guards, burglar bars, etc.), insurance and private counsel fees, bail bonds, and witness expenses. These private costs alone will average $9.2 billion. Upon totaling these costs, one will find that we are spending enough money per year on crime to represent the gross national product for many countries.

There are other crimes, committed daily in our society that are far more damaging and morally costly than those previously mentioned. These are crimes that are committed against human dignity and decency. These are crimes that deny the masses in society access to correct knowledge. For example, before a man is born into the world, he has already had false concepts of reality designed for him. Such false and confusing religious concepts as the teachings that "Jesus Christ died for your sins", "Man was born in sin", and a Caucasion image of Divine is labelled as "God the Father, God the Son and God the Holy Ghost". These are crimes against humanity and Allah Himself. These are destructive criminal influences that discourage the use of one's own intelligence. These influences prepare the peoples' minds to accept weakness as a way of life.

The great majority of the freakish crimes that occur in America are germinated by the crazy things that people are taught in religion, that they do not understand. For example, Jim Jones of the infamous Guyana "Jones Town" was attempting to dramatize an evil. He did not care if he sacrificed those people because the things that he had in his mind were so important to him that their lives were worthless in his plan. His main objective was to dramatize the evils and the hidden things of Scripture.

In our institutions of higher learning, young people are being encouraged to accept gambling, alcoholism, prostitution, and drug abuse as victimless crimes. The individual, the family, the community and the country suffer greatly because of these offenses. There is no such thing as a victimless crime—society is the victim. This is one of the many lies that have been used to create a false and deceptive environment in America. The American environment is

5

filled with these kinds of devastating lies. How can one develop naturally in a society when the climate is negative? These crimes, lies and weak ideas are planned to distort the human form. It is the moral crimes that have brought America to its present state of weakness. It is because of weak morals that crime is able to proliferate so rapidly. By denying the masses correct knowledge, they readily accept crime without question. Our country is morally bankrupt and is finding it very difficult to deal with other nations from a moral position. Hence, we are having problems with countries in the Middle East such as Palestine, Iran, Libya, Syria and others.

Crimes against the development of human society were, in part, addressed by the President's Commission Report in its conclusion:

> "Reducing poverty, discrimination, ignorance, disease and urban plight, and the anger, cynicism or despair those conditions can inspire, is one great step towards reducing crime. It is not the task, it is not within the competence of a Commission on Law Enforcement and Administration of Justice to make detailed proposals about housing or education or civil rights; unemployment or welfare or health. However, it is the Commission's clear and urgent duty to stress that forceful action in these fields is essential to crime prevention, and to adjure the officials in every agency of criminal justice— policemen, prosecutors, judges and correctional authorities to associate themselves with and labor for the success of the programs that will improve the quality of American life."

Here, President Johnson's Commission was addressing criminal neglect of the human being.

The environment for human development has been distorted to such an extent that some people feel that crime is a natural by-product of civilization. In other words, the citizens of America feel that crime in our society is as "American as an apple pie". Therefore, what appears to be a good and natural process of reasoning is, in reality, a trap that snares the unsuspecting person. What the masses may view as a logical conclusion may, in reality, be the blunder of the year.

Look briefly at how opinion polls are used to form opinions for the masses. Some of the methods used are, in reality, criminal acts. A miseducated public, that is also misinformed, can only seek to destroy itself and its leadership. How can rational movement be made, when that movement is based on the opinion of a miseducated and a misinformed public? Our Criminal Justice System presently functions in this manner. The political process that is used to select the managers that supervise our Criminal Justice System is shaped by public opinion. It is public opinion that oftentimes determines policy for the Criminal Justice System.

It is criminal to seek the opinion of a cross-section of the afore-mentioned public and, subsequently, flash the results of this poll across the country on national television, magazines, etc. The great majority of the public is swayed by these polls. These polls are used by unscrupulous people to gain leverage and power over the masses. How can the public oversee the Criminal Justice System, when it is ignorant of its responsibility both individually and collectively?

The importance of eliminating crime cannot be overemphasized, if we want America to survive. A recent Chicago Sun-Times news editorial indicated that a survey had been conducted of 61 Federal Bureau of Investigation's field offices around the country. This survey showed that the agents placed enormous emphasis on their concern for white collar crime. More than 50 percent of them con-sidered the corruption of public officials to be the "Public Enemy Number One". Processing criminals in America is big business, but it is a negative process. We should welcome the seeking of new avenues of employment for at least half of these employees that are presently in our Criminal Justice System. Yet, we are anticipating having to hire many more in the very near future.

We must continue to stress that the economic impact of crime must be measured in terms of its total cost to our society and the world. Criminal acts which cause property destruction or injury to persons, not only result in losses to the victims and their families, but they also result in the withdrawal of wealth and/or productivity from the economy as a whole.

Gambling is a criminal offense that produces additional wealth for organized crime. The proceeds that organized crime collects from gambling help to form major sources of income that organized hoodlums must have in order to achieve and exercise their economic and political power. The proceeds from gambling supply investment capital for organized crime. This money allows known thugs to make real property investments as well as banking investments and incorporate businesses, and engage in other lucrative and legitimate business endeavors. Hence, we have corruption in government and businesses.

The Holy Quran and Bible specifically condemn the practice of gambling. (Holy Quran, Chapter 5, Verses 93-94) Gambling and other games of chance cause man to deviate from his normal course of life. To invest one's abilities in the unpredictable turns of a wheel on a gambling table can create unnecessary strains on the nerves, and it creates foolhardiness in the individual. It creates unwarranted recklessness. A healthy society will not survive with a "gambling mentality". This insidious behavior is intended to entrap the mind, body and soul of the man and his society. This is a sly and subtle way of inducing a kind of recklessness in one's behavior.

Gambling actively cultivates a hit or miss kind of character. The very definition of the word gambling (an act or undertaking of uncertain outcome, or risk) demonstrates that this is not normal human behavior. The act of gambling occurs at all levels of our society; political, educational and cultural. This attitude of gambling should explain why we are still hitting and missing in our correctional system.

According to the U.S. National Commission on Criminal Justice Standards and Goals:

> "Mounting evidence of the ineffectiveness of correctional treatment programs for confined offenders has led to a new body of opinion about the role of the prison. This consensus holds that use of incarceration should be limited to the control of offenders from whom the public cannot be protected in any other way. It is further held that the changing of offenders into responsible citizens must take place in society, not behind prison walls."

It should be noted that under the present system, it is less costly to allow the criminal to remain free, as opposed to confining him to a maximum security institution. This statement strongly supports the opinion of Imam Warith Deen Muhammad. He stated that a man in prison today has to be separated from other men of like criminal propensities. A man convicted and confined to prison for any crime should not be allowed to associate with other criminals unless he is under strict supervision by morally strong people. He should be isolated and taught by morally upright correctional officers.

Due to the prohibitive cost factor and the consistent findings that our present treatment programs are not effective in dealing with rehabilitating confined offenders, many States have reorganized their correctional services. Many members of the Bench and the Bar have changed their views about the disposition of offenders. They know that incarceration is simply not the total solution to crime. But, they also understand that the Nation will have to support prisons for many years because society must be protected. This is a reality that we all must face. There are some people in our socity that must be put to death or incarcerated upon finding them guilty, if society is to survive. According to New Jersey Governor Brendon T. Byrne, Chairman of the National Advisory Committee on Criminal Justice Standards, the U.S. Task Force for Criminal Justice has spent $100 million each year during the past decade for research and develop-

8

ment. This means that the American taxpayers have been forced to pay over $1 billion over the past ten years to researchers who have not yet come up with solutions. We are getting good statistics, but no solutions. According to Byrne, this work is performed by grantees and contractors in universities, non-profit institutions, and private industry. This Task Force report also acknowledges that the details of research, design and methods normally are beyond the interest or expertise of the policymakers. If the policymakers are not interested, or perhaps do not understand how the studies were conducted, how can they intelligently apply the findings? How can they determine the validity of the research? Without interest, man is not motivated.

In private industry, an investment of $1.2 billion over a ten-year period would demand a reasonable return in the form of profits or increased production. It appears that the only return that the taxpayers are going to get is an opportunity to pay it again. What is the purpose of research, if it is not providing solutions to the problems? The research is simply magnifying or amplifying the problems. It is amazing that our government can allow such an expenditure in this field and it has yet to consider the solutions applied by the American Muslim Mission (A.M.M.) The A.M.M. has led every group in America in the field of social reform. No one has matched its accomplishments in the social reform of the human being. The A.M.M. has presented its methods of success to various criminal justice institutions and to other social thinkers who are aware of the impact that the religion of Al-Islam has had on the Criminal Justice System. The A.M.M. still challenges the researchers to evaluate the influence of Al-Islam, as it relates to this particular social problem. Their unbiased research will disclose clearly, without reservations, that the application of the principles of this way of life (Al-Islam) can bring about positive and revolutionary changes within the Criminal Justice System.

A nation-wide survey conducted in 1976 by the U.S. Law Enforcement Assistance Administration reveals that an estimated 191,400 persons legally classified as either adult or youthful offenders were being held in custody under the jurisdiction of State correctional authorities. Of these, 187,500 or 98 percent were sentenced inmates. The remainder represented unsentenced inmates, including persons committed for study and observation prior to sentencing, persons awaiting trial or release on bail, and persons being held for other authorities. It has been estimated, by the way, that it costs about $14,000 per year to sustain each inmate. This cost varies depending on the method used to calculate the cost.

9

Of this number of inmates, female prisoners represented only about 3 percent. The overwhelming majority were males. The Caucasian inmates making up approximately 51 percent of the total outnumbered members of other racial groups. The Bilalians made up 47 percent of the prison population, yet the Bilalian represents only 11 percent of the civilian population in the U.S. These statistics should raise questions in the Bilalian communities.

All except about one percent of the total number of prison inmates were 18 years and older. Twenty-five percent of all prisoners were 18 to 34 years old, yet, only 40 percent of the males 18 and older in the general civilian population were in this age category.

One may view these statistics in another way. Nearly one-half of our national State prison population consists of Bilalian inmates. In other words, nearly 90,000 Bilalians were incarcerated for felony offenses in 1974. If past statistics are an indication, this figure has since increased by about 20 percent. This is an indictment against our society in general and an indictment against the Bilalian leadership in particular.

Of this total number of inmates incarcerated, 116,500 or 61 percent used drugs. Whereas, 39 percent or 74,500 stated that they had never used drugs. Approximately 50,600 or 43 percent of these inmates were under the influence of drugs at the time they committed the offense for which they were being incarcerated.

Under the National Manpower Survey conducted, we found that the Criminal Justice System necessitated the employment of nearly one million persons. Over 580,000 were employed in the police protection agencies, of whom about 80 percent were sworn officers. Some 190,000 were in courts, prosecution and legal services, and indigent defense agencies, including about 28,000 judges and other judicial officers. We employed about 21,000 prosecutors, assistant prosecutors and other attorneys in prosecution and legal services offices, and 4,000 defenders or assistant defenders (public defenders).

The national State correctional agencies claimed 220,000 personnel members from the original one million employees. This figure includes about 70,000 correctional officers in adult facilities, 18,000 child caseworkers, 23,000 probation and parole officers, and 23,000 treatment and education specialists of all types.

Based on a poll taken of these agencies and their executives, there is a need to increase the overall criminal justice personnel by 220,000 or 26 percent. The largest shortages were reported by probation and parole administrators of juvenile corrections agencies.

Again, these statistics demonstrate rather dramatically how crime is affecting our society at all levels. We are burdened not only by the monetary drain, but also by the great loss in human resources. Here we have a need to utilize nearly 1.2 million citizens to either regulate, alter or nullify the behavior of an increasing number of our citizens due to criminal activity. This number easily represents the total population in many countries in the world.

Expenditures for the Criminal Justice System increased from $4.61 billion in 1965 to $17.2 billion in fiscal 1975. The newly released criminal justice expenditure totals for 1976 showed a figure of nearly $20 billion. This figure, according to advance reports, indicates that we are paying almost as much for our Criminal Justice System as we are paying for our health and hosiptals. The health and hospital costs in 1975 were about $24.8 billion.

We now realize that due to the nature of crime, and the manner in which it affects the total social order, we cannot readily place a monetary cost on it. We have also learned that the social destruction that takes place is far more costly than material loss or gain.

This chapter was designed to increase our concern about the problem of crime. It is also constructed to promote serious thinking among those readers who are sincerely dedicated to correcting our Criminal Justice System. This chapter should also give the taxpayer some insight as to how much of our public monies are being misused.

The following chapters will seek to answer many of the perplexing and heretofore unanswered questions about crime and what we can do to solve the problems of crime in America.

# CHAPTER 2

# HOW CRIMINAL BEHAVIOR IS DEFINED

## Part I

## Special Interests Define Criminal Behavior

Criminal behavior has been historically defined by powerful and selfish interest groups in America and in other Western societies. This problem may not have been previously considered by some, but it is a reality. In a highly politically organized society, one that is devoid of the correct guidance of Allah (God), powerful special interest groups develop. These groups are not primarily interested in the human concerns of man. For example, a large corporation like the Penn Central Railroad or even larger multi-national corporations such as AT&T (American Telephone and Telegraph) represent powerful special interest groups that are primarily concerned with profits. Business conglomerates such as these do provide very necessary goods and services for humanity. But their real interest is directed towards showing an increase in profits at the end of each fiscal quarter. In some instances, the service delivered will decrease, but the cost of delivery for the consumer will increase. There are approximately 500 huge industrial corporations that dominate the business world. Source: (Stephen Hymer and Robert Rowthors—Multi-national Corporations and International Oligopoly: The Non-American Challenge, M.I.T. Press, 1970. Other references: Massachusetts Institute of Technology). Of these corporations, 300 are in the United States and 200 are non-U.S. businesses. However, these huge corporations have interlocking Boards of Directors, thereby maintaining and controlling the political power within their spheres. These multi-national corporations can define criminal behavior in many ways and in many countries. For example, if a corporation purchases land to build a power plant, a huge factory or a railroad, laws will have to be established and enforced to protect these investments. Hence, the natives living in these areas, who were heretofore free to have access to these lands, would subsequently have what was once normal behavior declared as criminal. The plight of the American Indian today is a classic example of a people whose normal behavior was defined as criminal by special interest groups. Special interest groups assisted in financing the colonization of America. Laws were enacted to prevent the native American (Indians) from having access to land that they had historically lived on.

The most unique example of all that demonstrates how powerful special interest groups define criminal behavior among the masses of people is the Bilalian (African American) experience. The history of slavery eloquently speaks to this theory of how powerful special interest groups are able to get their interests converted into laws that, in turn, enable them to dominate and control the very lives and destiny of human beings. This insidious practice is still very much in effect, but, it is carried out in a more subtle manner.

For example, laws and ordinances are constantly altered by special interest groups to frustrate the efforts of the American voters to obtain open government, thereby assuring themselves of ultimately living in a true democracy. How else can one explain the existence of such groups as the Independent Voters of America, the Alliance to End Repression, the N.A.A.C.P., The League Of Women Voters, etc.?

One realizes that criminal laws are necessary, but one must also ask the question, are criminal laws the fruit of powerful and selfish interests that exclude the genuine and universal concerns of the human being? Or, are criminal laws the fruit of revealed knowledge, knowledge directly from God through His Prophets, especially through his last prophet Muhammad (P.B.U.H.)? That is, knowledge that will allow mankind to establish a just and righteous society? It is obvious to many that laws in America are not being formulated or enforced in the spirit of justice and righteousness. Upon examining the profile of the inmate population in our correctional system, one must conclude that the thrust of criminal laws and their enforcement is directed towards the masses.

On any given day in America, one will find approximately one million males locked up in our national correctional system. Of this number, only 1.1 percent has 4 years or more of college, 40.3 percent has only 5 to 8 years of elementary schooling, and 27.6 percent completed 1 to 3 years of high school.

To put it another way, roughly 79 percent of the felony inmates in America did not finish high school, and of this percentage, almost 90 percent never went to high school. A close study of this profile and a similar study of the community profile from whence the inmates came will show a striking resemblance. This resemblance will be high population density, poor education, lack of political power and little economic or cultural strength. It is no accident that the Bilalian (African American) is represented within the inmate population by a highly disproportionate percentage. One will also find that his community (Bilalian community) represents the highest rate of unemployment and the lowest rate of economic stability within the confines of America.

According to a recent survey in the **U.S. News and World Report** magazine, April 14, 1980 issue, the following chart depicted the institutions which wield the most influential power. Of the 30 listed, none of them, with the exception of the American Muslim Mission, under "religion", has consistently attacked the root causes of the great social problems facing humanity today. This includes "The White House", "Television", "Large Businesses", etc. According to the survey, television is the second most influential institution in America. Why hasn't it assumed its role of supporting humanity's struggle for justice and the elimination of crime by reordering priorities? This institution has yet to use its great influence in a positive way. It will show an hour of positive activities that promotes healthy human aspirations and goals, as contrasted with 23 hours of pornography, violence, games of chance and sporting events.

# Institutions: Which Wield the Most Power?

*Persons taking part in the survey were asked to assess 30 U.S. institutions "according to the amount of influence you think it has on decisions affecting the nation as a whole." Each institution could be ranked from 1 to 7—1 meaning very little influence and 7 very great. The outcome:*

| The Most Influential | Average Rating |
|---|---|
| 1. The White House | 6.34 |
| 2. Television | 5.75 |
| 3. Large business | 5.73 |
| 4. Oil industry | 5.49 |
| 5. Supreme Court | 5.48 |
| 6. U.S. Senate | 5.46 |
| 7. Bank | 5.42 |
| 8. Federal bureaucracy | 5.37 |
| 9. Lobby and pressure groups | 5.29 |
| 10. Labor unions | 5.28 |

| Other Rankings | Average Rating |
|---|---|
| 11. U.S. House | 5.25 |
| 12. Newspapers | 4.90 |
| 13. Wall Street | 4.87 |
| 14. Cabinet | 4.58 |
| 15. Public-opinion polls | 4.47 |
| 16. Democratic Party | 4.27 |
| 17. Radio | 4.25 |
| 18. Advertising | 4.24 |
| 19. Legal profession | 4.10 |
| 20. Magazines | 4.07 |
| 21. State and local governments | 3.97 |
| 22. Military | 3.94 |
| 23. Educational institutions | 3.86 |
| 24. Civil-rights groups | 3.73 |
| 25. Medical profession | 3.44 |
| 26. Family | 3.43 |
| 27. Republican Party | 3.22 |
| 28. Organized religion | 3.21 |
| 29. Small business | 2.95 |
| 30. Cinema | 2.90 |

U.S. NEWS & WORLD REPORT, April 14, 1980

The definition of crime, as it is presently applied to behavior, must be redefined. Criminal behavior cannot be defined primarily to support and protect selfish and corrupt interests. Criminal behavior has to be rightfully defined as any behavior that is contrary to the will of Almighty God, Allah. This behavior is not prescribed for all mankind through the life example of Prophet Muhammad. The Holy Quran was revealed to Prophet Muhammad to serve as a "manual", a guide with specific instructions for mankind.

Therefore, our first priority should be to redefine criminal behavior along the guidelines established by Allah through his Prophet Muhammad. By using these guidelines, one arrives at the conclusion that the worst crime that man can commit is to associate anything with God. It is through associating other things, for example, persons, wealth, power, etc., with God that man has brought so much corruption into his society.

In summary, one must conclude that it is because of the behavior of powerful, corrupt and selfish interest groups that large numbers of poor people have become criminals. The average offender that is in our Criminal Justice System today did not have much of a choice. The offender may have been found guilty by a court of law and he probably did in fact commit the crime for which he is being punished. But he had very little choice in the direction in which he was traveling.

The powerful, influential groups in America have failed to bring their powers to bear on racism, poverty, and injustice. They have stood by and subtly encouraged negative behavior so that their positions will remain intact.

Another powerful interest group that has effectively converted its interests into criminal laws and other laws affecting the people of society is the Church. Huge blocks of people (nations) around the world are held in check by the influence of religion. Religion is the most powerful influence in man's life.

Religious institutions exert pressures on their followers that may determine where one lives, who one may marry, one's diet, or where one may be buried after death. The Church may also determine one's source of income, moral values, and one's political, social, educational, and cultural behavior.

Once the people accept a religious doctrine, it becomes the mechanism for producing the laws of the land. Here the Church has moved into the position of defining criminal behavior. When the people came under the influence of Christianity and accepted the concept of original sin, they also accepted to be defined as criminals.

Hence, since this concept tells the people that they are born in sin, Christianity has defined man's birth as being an act of criminal behavior.

According to the Bible, Christianity teaches its followers that they are born in sin, they are shaped in iniquity, and they must accept Jesus Christ, the "Son of God", as their Savior. This catechism reinforces the fact that the Church has defined man's birth and his very existence as criminal behavior.

It has been predetermined that the special interest groups in the field of economics are primarily concerned with defining criminal behavior in order to protect their financial interests. What is the logic behind the Christian Church's definition of criminal behavior (man is born in sin)? Who will benefit if the followers accept this concept? Will it be the people or will it be the Church?

Psychology has taught us that if one accepts to be inferior and internalizes his inferiority, he will begin to act out this perception of himself. Therefore, one can or must conclude that criminal behavior is not only defined by Christianity, but it is also promoted by the Church. Why should man strive to be an upright and morally strong citizen in his community after being told by the most influential body in the country that he was born wicked and is inclined to do wrong? Man can easily rationalize why he breaks established laws, when he is under the influence of Christianity. Many times we have heard the expression that "the devil made me do it".

## Part II

## The Influence of Judaism and Christianity in Defining Criminal Behavior

The theory that Christian influence has promoted crime is not difficult to understand after examining some of its concepts and religious practices. We must also consider the origin of Christianity. We must examine how it originated from a corrupt form of Judaism and began to promote racial superiority among some people and racial inferiority among others.

Purity of worship in religion is an absolute necessity if man is to survive as a strong moral being. Corrupt religious concepts have prevented this kind of development. Corrupt religion has fragmented the total organic structure of the human being. The human being is structured as an intellectual being, physical being, and, ultimately, a spiritual being. If these component parts are not coordinated properly during man's development, he may place more emphasis on intellectual growth than on his moral growth, or he may place more emphasis on material growth (wealth) than on spiritual growth.

A close examination of the behavior of men that administer the previously discussed multi-national corporations will disclose that they too are influenced by religious institutions. Yet, the moral influence of these institutions is not strong enough to eliminate their greed and lust for power. In fact, man's greed and lust for power has been promoted by false religious concepts and influences.

The religion of Orthodox Judaism cannot stand the test of purity of worship. Because purity of worship will guide man in the development of a just society. We can safely say that Orthodox Judaism has fallen short. Orthodox Jewish concepts have been used down through the ages, and very effectively, to rule and control the world masses. These concepts were used to define criminal behavior in the same manner as we have previously discussed.

Here again, emphasis must be placed on the fact that religion normally exerts the greatest influence on man's behavior. It is man's perception of what is most important in his life that will determine his behavior and his relationship with other people. If he places anything above human dignity for all men, his religious orientation is not balanced with the reality of creation or his own human nature.

Hence, man is able to commit crimes against other men in society by overcharging them for inferior products, refusing to pay a man a just wage, or denying others access to the knowledge, etc., without feeling any pains of guilt. This type of man is usually able to justify his behavior through religious concepts. His claim may be that God has blessed him to be in whatever position that he is in, therefore, he has a right to manage his authority or his wealth in any manner that he deems fit.

This is a kind of "survival of the fittest" mentality that is very prevalent in America. This attitude can easily be traced back to religious concepts that are in the Bible. It is said in some parts of the Bible that Jewish people are to be the inheritors of the land, and that the people of these lands are to be their servants. The Orthodox Jew's claim of being God's chosen people formed the foundation upon which was built the social, economic and political structure that enabled a handful of Satan's disciples to dominate the world by defining criminal behavior—both legal and illegal activity.

This claim (God's chosen people) by the Orthodox Jews has been accepted by the great majority of the world's people. Hence, the people of the world have accepted to be inferior. This concept

17

promotes racism and debasement in man. The European was given this doctrine through Christianity and, subsequently, rule by racial claims of superiority has been the order of the day. The whole of Christianity in the world today is based on the destructive concept of racism. Study the consistent use of Caucasian images of Divine that are prominently displayed wherever Christianity is taught. There are images of saints, the Prophet Jesus (peace be upon him), and Mary displayed in most churches in America, and these images have predominately Caucasian features. Most pictures of Jesus depict a Caucasian man who is also said to be God the Father, God the Son and God the Holy Ghost. Where does this leave the people of color? This form of racial inferiority has been methodically fed into the minds of the people of color ever since the inception of Christianity. The special interest of the Church, under this satanic leadership, was to bring the world masses under its complete control.

This kind of teaching (indoctrination) is aimed at the destruction of the whole human race. It uses the Caucasian people as a tool to psychologically relegate mankind to certain positions or classes beneath the Caucasian in the eyes of God. It makes all men of color inferior in the eyes of God, and it makes the Caucasian superior. Anyone who accepts these false concepts has fallen prey to the aforementioned Jahcubite conspirators.

The correctional system should seriously examine the design shown in these previous paragraphs that demonstrates how religion has influenced criminal behavior. This examination should be conducted with a view of learning how one can best utilize this knowledge to affect change within the system. We cannot conceivably correct any inmate or offender without first correcting our own false images of reality.

The leader of the A.M.M. began to direct our attention to this corrupt process of defining criminal behavior nearly seven years ago. Imam Warith Deen Muhammad has repeatedly emphasized the necessity to eliminate the racial images from worship. In the A. M. Journal newspaper he outlines the plot in this manner. "A Message of Concern to the American People":

> "Harmful pagan influence was sneaked in on the 'Gentiles' by the Jahcubites, who were looking for political and material dominance over the world. They gave them such a religion so that they would worship a Deliverer in their own image, but a Deliverer tied to the Jahcubite people. Many Jews are against Jahcubism."

Jahcubism is a term coined by Imam Warith Deen Muhammad to describe the personality of a man with a satanic mind. Satan is not

18

racist; he will dominate any man regardless of his ethnicity, if he is allowed to do so.

Our leader, Imam Warith Deen Muhammad, went on to describe the harmful seductive **message** that this scheme was designed to deliver. He said:

> "You can't live in America without hearing the message. The message of white supremacy is everywhere. You are conscious that Jesus is in a white body even if you don't go to church. Every American knows that Jesus is put into a 'white', European image by church society. Every American knows that the apostles and saints and angels are made European by church society.
>
> " You don't have to be consciously aware of it as a 'white' Jesus or as a 'white' religion. The very fact that our minds exist in this environment is enough to make that image and those messages go into our subconscious and cripple Bila- lian ('Black') people's ability to lift themselves up out of inferiority. It also keeps Caucasian peoples' minds in a false world by preventing them from seeing their real worth and values as human beings apart from their physical skin color."

This false idolatrous worship causes many poorly educated people to overcrowd the jails and prisons in America. The very definition of idolatry means blind admiration or devotion to idols, that is, to something visible but without substance. It is plain to see that once a people have been steeped in this kind of religious worship, they will give themselves to any destructive influence that comes along.

The influence of Christianity in the lives of Bilalian people has produced more crime and aberrant behavior among this ethnic group than any other people. Christianity has nurtured an identity crisis among this group that is peculiar only to the Bilalian people. It is impossible to find another ethnic group of people suffering so deeply (psychologically, socially and culturally) from this problem.

Crime within the Bilalian community is an acting out of self- hatred which has been encouraged by a false Christian doctrine. It is impossible, under this present influence, for the Bilalian to view himself as anything but an inferior being. It is very easy for an 18-year-old Bilalian male to brutally assault and rob an 84-year-old Bilalian woman or any woman for that matter, because he views himself, subconsciously, as being less than human. This perception of one's own inferiority can very easily, in time, be transferred through the mind's eye to a similar perception of other human beings.

19

When we examine the behavior of Bilalian people who have not been identified as criminals, we find that they too actively engage in character assassinations and backbiting among themselves. Unity within this community is completely lacking due to the weak self-image that Christianity has given it.

# CHAPTER 3

# THE CREATOR OF CRIME

Crime is a false creation of man. It is abnormal behavior that develops when man comes under the influuence of false, corrupt knowledge. Man, by nature, is not criminal. However, some theorists have suggested that man is selfish by nature, due to the behavior he exhibits as a child. But as we know, man grows out of his childish behavior with normal maturity. As a child, a man is similar to a plant. It simply seeks whatever nutrients it needs for sustenance and is not concerned about the welfare of other plants. This is the nature of the plant. The nature of the baby is similar with exceptions; the main one being the child has a loving, human nature. It has sentiments and needs affection.

The original nature of the human being is to be loving, kind and compassionate; innocent and devoid of vanity, selfishness and greed. In the Quran, Allah tells man that he is created in the best image and in the best form. This is quite contrary to what the Bible tells man. Man enters the world innocent of any corruption. His mind is not distorted until he is impacted by a distorted environment. The environment teaches the man to be a liar and a thief, a homosexual and a pervert, a corrupt businessman, or a corrupt political leader.

The world of humanity has consistently displayed compassion under some of the most trying conditions. This clearly demonstrates that man has a natural propensity to be kind and loving. Morality is still the number one factor that commands respect in the community of man. Therefore, the view that man is criminal by nature has to be rejected. The human being stands ever ready to sacrifice himself for almost any cause; thereby further demonstrating his lack of selfishness. Man has been misguided to the extent that he does not know what to sacrifice himself for or to whom he should give himself. This behavior cannot be attributed to the view that man is naturally sinful; but, because man has strayed away from the guidance of God, he has no realistic direction for his life. It is through this process of misguidance that man becomes actively engaged in criminal behavior. To misguide implies some kind of deception or scheme.

The creator of crime is a mentality that seeks dominance over the world. This Jahcubite mentality rises to power through lies and deceit. Its nourishment is derived from lies. It encourages its followers and supporters to engage in the practice of building lies and

21

creating false images. The creator of crime lays the foundation for the masses to commit criminal acts and then punishes them for getting caught. There is no law against practicing crime in America, but there is a law against getting caught.

Satan (the creator of crime) develops by using his intellect. He refuses to submit to the dictates of his heart. He disobeys his original nature, which is to submit to his heart (righteousness). The dictates of the heart are naturally regulated with one's intellect, thereby giving man the balance that he needs. Satan is not concerned with the dictates of the heart. The Criminal Justice System in America has been geared to function in an imbalanced manner, very similar to that of a man who has no balance. The system is devoid of heart (sincere concern). It responds to problems intellectually and rationally without moral concerns.

Al Islam teaches man that he was created with an original nature. This original nature guides man toward perfection. The human being is created with a desire to have a strong moral character, to pursue excellence in all of his endeavors, to deal fairly with his fellow man, to seek strong and just family ties as well as a strong community life. If the criminal justice system would accept this simple concept, study it and apply it, we would begin to solve some of our problems. This is wisdom that is far better than science.

In June 1983 the warden at Pontiac State Prison fell into one of the traps of Satan because he was either ignorant or he doesn't accept the guidance of God. This warden allowed a filthy pornographic movie to be shown to the inmates on closed circuit television for a full 90 minutes. Don't we have enough problems with devrate sex in the prison system? Are we really concerned about the welfare of the human being?

The correctional system has to focus its attention on the satanic influences that produce and label criminal behavior in order to successfully carry out its responsibiilties of rehabilitation. Correction is a science that can be perfected. But, in order to do so, one must apply knowledge and wisdom that is even more exact than science; that is, wisdom and knowledge from Allah, Himself. The mentality that creates crime cannot be taken lightly. It is the Jahcubite personality that makes war against human development.

When the ruling class assumes that only it should determine man's destiny, and it should control man's life, it has taken on the mind of the devil, itself. Anyone who accepts this kind of religious philosophy takes on the same mentality. Consequently, there is a group of people in this American society who really feel that they have complete control over the masses, and the people and its institutions have no choice but to follow their dictates. The correctional system must realize that it too is under this kind of satanic, cold, illogical (Author: logical implies natural order), pseudointellectual rule. One should realize that this mentality is quite capable of implementing innovative changes within the correctional system whenever it desires to do so. But, these changes are not designed to solve problems in corrections; they are designed to increase them or magnify them.

How else can one explain the rapid increase in crime and the subsequent increase in correctional problems? Even though we have more professional people working in corrections today than we have ever had, and we spend more money and have more programs, America's problems with corrections have increased. The Bible speaks of evil thinking people being located in the holiest of places.

This concept, of evil thinking people being found in the holiest of places, symbolizes the fact that there are evil influences controlling the behavior of many individuals who are in various positions of authority. The public may assume that simply because a man has been appointed to the position of warden, director of corrections, the pastor of a church etc., he is an honest man who will seek to perform his job in an honorable way. This is not always true.

On the contrary, the higher a man/woman moves up in the management or governing mechanism of our society, the greater pressures he/she will experience from morally corrupting influences. And if they do not have strong faith in God and remain morally strong, they will subsequently yield to the influences of Satan and begin to work against humanity.

The correctional system has to wake up to the reality of who is creating crime and how it is being perpetrated. It has to have the courage to speak out against the wicked mind. The correctional system has but to examine its operations and it will find that it is aiding Satan in creating crime. Our correctional facilities are actual breeding grounds for crime, homosexual conduct, and racism. A **Bilalian News/A.M. Journal** article entitled "The Vampires of Vacaville" (September 12, 1980), pointed out that the Vacaville, California Prison for Males was being used as a laboratory to promote and study homosexuality.

According to the author, Vacaville caters to its homosexual population in nearly every area. Those inmates (homosexuals) who go to Vacaville are treated with hormones to make them more effeminate, to increase their breast sizes, and to make their hair longer in some cases. The author also states that there are countless cases of "straight men" and homosexuals being "married" by staff officials at Vacaville. . . .

Some prison guards complained, upon being interviewed, that they were unable to enforce the rules laid down by their central office in Sacramento. The author was told that officers who catch people engaged in sexual acts are discouraged from reporting what they see on the "rules violation report". There have also been cases of prison guards being caught in compromising situations with homosexual inmates.

The creator of crime has grown in such proportions that he has turned the correctional system into a "corruptional system". That is to say that law violators enter our correctional system for punishment and rehabilitation, but a greater number leave the system as freaks or as distorted human beings.

# CHAPTER 4

# CORRECTIONAL FACILITIES IN AMERICA

The American correctional system is as diversified in its facilities, theories, techniques and programs as it is in its varied inmate sub-cultural groups. This system handles nearly 1.3 million offenders each day, and it has over 2.5 million admissions per year. (Source: The President's Commission on Law Enforcement and Administration of Justice. Task Force Report Corrections. P. I, Table 1).

Correctional functions are administered by Federal, State, County and Municipal Governments. Some have developed good programs for control and rehabilitation of offenders. But, most of them lack the ability to effectively deal with the problem of recidivism, i.e., the commission of additional crimes by the ex-offender after his/her release.

The average citizen has very little, if any, knowledge about the correctional system except that portion that they may have become involved in. Therefore, we will begin with a brief summary of the system as it operates today.

# Part I

# PEOPLE UNDER CORRECTIONAL AUTHORITY

Offenders in the correctional system are assigned to varying facilities and programs depending upon their ages, offense, psychological disposition, and design of the particular institutions. Some offenders may, subsequently, be assigned to juvenile institutions or juvenile community programs. The adult felons, that is, persons convicted of a crime and sentenced to serve over a year in a State or Federal penitentiary, may be institutionalized or placed on probation or put into a work release program. This same procedure would apply to the misdemeanants, i.e., persons guilty of minor offenses and sentenced to serve less than a year.

In some States, juveniles are processed as adults for some serious crimes. They, in turn, are held responsible as adults and are treated accordingly along with the adults. Normally, the great majority of juveniles are handled under special procedures. They are handled in juvenile courts under careful scrutiny and are referred to special correctional programs. There is a concerted effort to keep them separate from adults whenever possible to prevent them from coming under negative influences.

This is an obvious inconsistency. Here the correctional system, under pressure from society, is concerned about a juvenile offender being influenced by a hardened criminal. Why wasn't society concerned about the juvenile's mind being influenced by the negative aberrate television programs, or the acid rock music and materialistic fads that he/she was exposed to prior to their criminal behavior? It is this kind of inconsistency that must be reconciled. It is obvious that the juvenile offender is acting out learned and programmed behavior.

Correctional systems everywhere are required to provide some degree of special handling for mentally ill offenders. Smaller States have segregated quarters for mental cases, whereas, larger jurisdictions have provided special institutions for the mentally ill convicts.

Even though there is great diversity in corrections, certain traits predominate. About 95 percent of all offenders are male; most are young—ages ranging between 15 and 30. Juveniles make up almost a third of all offenders under treatment with 63,000 in institutions and 285,000 under community supervision during an average day. Many come from urban slums . Members of minority groups that suffer economic and social discrimination are arrested in disproportionate numbers. Life histories of most offenders are case studies of the ways in which social and economic factors contribute to crime and delinquency. Education, for example, is a good barometer for success in modern America. Over half of the adult felony inmates do not have a high school education. (Source: The President's Commission on Law Enforcement and Administration of Justice. Task Force Report Corrections, P. 2, Figure 1):.

There are about 570 institutions for adult felons in America ranging from some of the oldest and largest prisons in the world to forestry camps for 30 to 40 trusted inmates. Overcrowding and idleness are prominent features of some, along with brutality and corruption. Although most inmates of American correctional institutions come from urban areas, the institutions themselves are often located away from urban areas and even primary transportation routes. Reasons for such locations were diverse and, to a large extent, now outdated.

## Part II

# CORRECTIONAL INSTITUTIONS

Prisons designed for secure custody have been built of stone, steel and concrete. The fact that they were well-constructed is testified to by the observations that sixty-one ancient prisons are still in use. These 61 institutions were opened before 1900.

There are many large maximum security prisons still being used in America. The Directory of the American Correctional Association showed an average population of over 2,000 inmates in 21 prisons. Four of these have well over 4,000 inmates each. These are: San Quentin in California, the Illinois State Prison Complex at Joliet and Stateville, the Michigan State Prison at Jackson, and the Ohio State Penitentiary at Columbus. (Source: The President's Commission on Law Enforcement and Administration of Justice. Task Force Report Corrections, P. 4).

# Part III

# CORRECTIONAL STAFF

Over 101,000 people were employed in corrections on an average day in 1965. Project this figure with an overall increase of about 10% in 14 years and you have a conservative estimate of 133,000 people presently employed in corrections. This number of people would represent a sizeable town or city.

Their areas of assignment (job categories) are roughly as follows: 63,000 or 52 percent of all staff were custodial employees—guards, supervisors, and house parents. Another 34,000 or 28 percent were engaged in service or administrative functions. Thus, only 24,000 workers or 20 percent were primarily engaged in activities specifically designed as treatment.

These figures may be increased moderately because an additional number of teachers, caseworkers and vocational instructors have been added to the staff since 1965. There is still a shortage of qualified personnel in some areas because of the low salaries paid in the field of corrections. For example, in 1965, the median starting salary for custodial employees in adult instituitions was between $4,000 and $5,000 annually. These salaries have since been raised from $8,000 to $10,000 annually. Teachers, social workers and counselors were underpaid during this time also. Their salaries have been increased in the past 14 years, making the positions more attractive.

As indicated earlier, this Chapter was designed to give the reader a brief summary or description of corrections in America. Many details have been omitted and some of the figures given were drawn from the President's Commission Report on Corrections as of 1965. Other data was obtained from the U.S. Department of Justice, which produces the 1974 Advance Report on the Census of State Correctional Facilities. Projections can be made based on the population increase and the present rate of convictions and releases of inmates. It is certain that nothing has decreased. Crime has risen considerably and so has the inmate population.

For example: The State of Illinois has a total prison population of well over 11,000 inmates. Subsequently, this system is forced to parole a minimum of 500 inmates per month. This must be done in order to allow it to accommodate the incoming convicted felons. This situation has caused complaints to be made by citizens in a public housing project in Chicago. Community leaders in the Cabrini Green Housing Project pointed out that the rapid release of ex-felons was making life unbearable in their community.

The Director of the Illinois Correctional System, Michael P. Lane, indicated that the system had no choice but to release 500 inmates 90 days prior to the completion of their sentences because "we simply don't have room". The complaint was also made that the parolees and those who "maxed out" (completed their sentence) were not being given the required orientation to aid in their re-entry into the civilian population. Mr. Franzen's response to this complaint was that some of the parolees and those released would not benefit from the orientation anyway.

# CHAPTER 5

# CRIME IN POOR COMMUNITIES

## Part I

## The Most Likely Victims

According to the President's Commission, one of the most fully documented facts about crime is that the common, serious crimes that worry people most, i.e., murder, forcible rape, robbery, aggravated assault and burglary—happen most often in the slums of large cities. Study after study in many cities have traced the variations in the rates for these crimes. The results, with consistent regularity, show that the offenses, the victims and the offenders are found most frequently in the poorest and most deteriorated and socially disorganized areas of our cities. Studies by the Law Enforcement Assistance Administration show that the most likely victim of a crime is a young, poor and uneducated male Bilalian.

The Federal Bureau of Investigation has been charged with the responsibility of preparing an annual report called the Uniform Crime Report. In 1978, it published this report and entitled it "Crime in the United States". This document represents, in some respects, the darker sides of human behavior in America.

These annual reports are compiled through the cooperative efforts of over 15,000 law enforcement agencies across the nation. The Uniform Crime Reporting (U.C.R.) Program provides periodic assessments of crime in the United States, and it produces a fairly reliable set of criminal statistics for use in law enforcement administration, operation and management. Data from this program is also widely utilized by other professionals. Therefore, one should utilize this information whenever possible.

The U.C.R. strongly supports the argument that we are rapidly losing the war against crime. This report in 1978 indicated that someone in America is victimized every 3 seconds by crime. (See illustration, Chapter 1, Page 4.) An index offense is committed every 3 seconds. An index offense is murder and non-negligent manslaughter, forcible rape, robbery, aggravated assault, burglary, larceny, theft and motor vehicle theft. On a monthly basis, law enforcement agencies report these crime index offenses to the F.B.I. who, in turn, compile them as previously indicated.

According to the U.C.R., there were 19,121 incidents of murder and non-negligent manslaughter committed in 1977. The following year (in 1978) there were 19,555 similar incidents which showed an increase of 2.3%. According to this same report in 1978, December had a higher frequency of murder offenses than any other month of the year. Isn't it odd that during the month of the celebration of the birth of Jesus Christ (the Prince of Peace) there were more killings than any other month of the year? One will also find that there is more emotional stress and unnecessary anxiety exhibited by America's citizens during the month of December.

Of the total 19,555 incidents of murder and non-negligent manslaughter, there were 18,714 murders. Of this total, 10,111 or 54% were Caucasians and 8,201 or 43.8% were Bilalians (African Americans). Even though the Bilalian people represent approximately 12% of the civilian population, their deaths due to willful violence represent 43% of the murdered national population. These statistics also reveal that the Bilalian citizens kill their own people with far more regularity than Caucasians.

Of the 8,201 Bilalians killed in 1978, only about 300 or 4% were murdered by Caucasians and members of other ethnic groups. The remainder, 7,901 or 96%, were murdered by other Bilalians. As we examine the statistics of other index crimes, we find the same pattern emerging. The most socially oppressed people, the people with the weakest cultural ties and poorest ethnic identity are most likely to be victimized by physical assaults and thefts than any other people in America. And, ironically, the described people are most likely to victimize themselves.

Many arguments can be made in defense of the Bilalian community's crime problems, but the arguments are not valid if the blame is to be placed on simple racism, i.e., racial oppression by Caucasian people. Unemployment is a factor that enters into the crime equation, and double standards of justice are an undeniable fact in America's Criminal Justice System as well as in its social life. But, these drawbacks as well as others not mentioned, do not justify the unnatural criminal behavior and self-hatred exhibited within the Bilalian community.

This previously described behavior has begun to filter out of the Bilalian community and into Caucasian America. We can now see Caucasian crime is on the increase. We have mentioned earlier how the drug problem is no longer an exclusive Bilalian problem. The influence and use of drugs has decimated many families and communities in Caucasian neighborhoods.

William H. Webster, the Director of the Federal Bureau of Investigation, said that "Studies exist which indicate that the educational levels and requisite training of police officers have dramatically improved over the years, better preparing those empowered to enforce the law . . . ; but, delegation of this problem to law enforcement agencies, however professional, has not been enough. Unless we as citizens, collectively and individually, join the crusade against crime, the vast resources of our respective governments will apparently have little or no effect on this nation's crime situation."

Here we are being told by the head of one of the leading and most respected law enforcement bodies in America that we are not doing enough. We are also told that we must respond from the community level and work hand in hand with law enforcement if we are to make any inroads towards the solution of this nation's crime problem. The only way that the community can come together in unity to work against crime or any problem is to unify under the most common and logical banner.

Studies relative to the distribution of crime rates in cities and the conditions of life most commonly associated with high crime rates have been conducted for well over a century in Europe and for many years in the United States. The findings have been consistent. Burglary, robbery and serious assaults occur more frequently in areas characterized by low income, physical deterioration, dependency, racial and ethnic concentrations, broken homes, working mothers, low levels of education and vocational skills, high unemployment, high proportions of single males, overcrowded and substandard housing, high rates of tuberculosis and other such similar traits that identify the poor masses in inner cities. Examine the statistics at the end of this Chapter. These will give a clear picture of the disproportionate rate of crimes committed by Bilalians against Bilalians. These are arrest and sentencing statistics for specific offenses based on race.

Crime rates tend to be highest in the center of our cities and decrease in relationship to the distance from the city. We know that our inner cities are primarily occupied by Bilalians (African Americans) and Spanish-American people. Upon studying this phenomenon, it is logical to conclude that this large degree of antisocial behavior that is uniquely peculiar to the poor in inner cities in America is not accidental. Dr. M. Harvey Brenner, an economist at Johns Hopkins University, found that for every one percent increase in the national unemployment rate, property crimes rise at an average rate of six percent, while homicides increase as much as four percent. Furthermore, he noted that the reverse is true—when unemployment goes down, so too does the crime rate. (Source: Ebony Magazine, Auguust, 1979, P. 72, Johnson Publication,

Chicago, Illinois). As we proceed in this work, we will show this criminal and antisocial behavior was encouraged among the poor by design and is not just a circumstantial happening.

In the areas identified by statistics as high crime rate areas, one will find more alcoholic liquors being sold per capita. It should strike the reader as being rather odd that one will find more taverns and liquor stores among the poor than you will find anywhere in America. There is no question about alcohol and its relationship to crime, unemployment, poor health, etc. Why then are alcoholic beverages made so readily available to the people who have already been identified as poorly educated, low in vocational skills, poorly structured socially and unable to rationally defend themselves against an oppressive environment? We also find that the poor and the ignorant are more likely to be victimized by criminal behavior and are the most likely to be arrested for criminal behavior. Crime and arrest situations occur far more frequently when alcohol is consumed either by the victim or the offender.

Narcotics and other dangerous drugs are more readily available to high school and grammar school students living in poverty areas (poorer communities). Students are selling drugs in many American schools with impunity. You have but to gain the confidence of any student in the inner city, and most likely he will be able to relate to you the drug selling activities of some of his fellow classmates. Local police statistics will verify this statement.

Crime in the poor communities is also aggravated by that lack of conscious human concern shown by the Civil Service workers, i.e., policemen, social workers, firemen, etc. It has been documented that the police use their discretionary powers of arrest and enforcement according to the neighborhood or community. The National Council on Crime and Delinquency in New York concluded in 1963 that, although arrests of Bilalian children were only 5.7 percent of the total juvenile arrests, these cases constituted 10.5 percent of the total court referrals. This study also indicated that arrests of Bilalian children are more frequently referred to court than arrests of Caucasian children. This difference in the rates of referral of arrests of Bilalian children is largely a result of more frequent referral of minor offenses of Bilalian children, according to this study. In other words, a Bilalian child is more likely to be referred to court for a minor offense than a Caucasian child for a similar charge. (Source: The Ambivalent Force; Xerox College Publishing. Niederhoffer Blumberg). When dealing with the juveniles in one area, the police officer may affect an arrest, but, in another part of the city, he may give the juvenile a pass.

32

Regardless of how the community is organized, the police still attempt to accomplish their job within the context of the community. What does the community expect the policemen to do? In some instances, the officer will ignore the prescribed legal process and attempt to conform to community expectations. (Source: William J. Chambliss & John T. Liell "The Legal Process in the Community Setting" Crime & Delinquency, 12 October, 1966, pp. 310-317).

For example, the citizens living in poor communities expect harsh treatment from the local police and the police inturn rise to the expectations of the people.

I personally recall going into homes as a police officer on family disturbance calls, and being confronted by irrate citizens. Some will attempt to provoke the officer into committing acts of violence against them. I have received such requests as "shoot me," or I have had statements directed at me such as, "I'm ready to die," or "you came here to beat me up anyway, so go ahead and do it." I have seen youths mockingly "spread eagle" against buildings or automobiles when the police drive by in their squad cars. We wouldn't have to stop the car or challenge them in any way. They would do this as a joke and also as a way of ridiculing the police, their methods and attitudes. This kind of behavior can be provocative to police officers who are motivated by false community expectations.

The Chicago police department represents the second largest local law enforcement agency in the country. It is viewed by many criminal justice authorities as one of the most progressive agencies as well. Yet the manner in which this department functions within the Bilalian and other poor communities encourages or promotes crime as opposed to being the deterrent that it should be. For example, the youth and the detective divisions of the Chicago police department have systematically eliminated the majority of its Bilalian officers and replaced them with their Caucasian counterparts. These (Caucasian) officers have demonstrated historically their insensitivity to the human concerns as well as the aspirations of the Bilalian community.

Consequently, members of this community, both youths and adults, are dealt with in an overly harsh and racist manner. The language used by the police vividly points out how negative feelings are generated within this community. The arrestees are often referred to as "heads."

This process of verbal dehumanization has been subsequently transformed into inhuman treatment of citizens by many police officers in Bilalian and poor areas of the city.

Many times youths are indiscriminately stopped and frisked

33

simply because the officer is looking for "heads" and he is oblivious of the fact that he is dealing with human beings. The officer is given a higher efficiency rating if he makes a physical arrest, regardless of the charge. In the latter part of the sixties the Chicago police department developed a "Gang Intelligence Unit." This unit, born with noble aims and purposes, has since expanded into practically an independed police force within the police department.

Since 1971 to the present, this "arm" of the police department has generated far more criminal activity than it can ever hope to deter or quell. Its corrupt and unchecked methods of operations within the Bilalian community and others, has produced more racial enmity than Chicago has had in a long time. And this unit has produced a deep seated distrust for Caucasian police officers in particular and the police department in general.

The Chicago police department is a classical model of how civil service agencies are generally insensitive in their dealings with the poor and the neglected. This agency reflects the mentality and the behavior of most police agencies in America. It is also an example of how the police are used to "over police" the impoverished and densely populated areas of America. When there are too many police officers assigned to patrol areas of this description, the citizens within these areas become agitated. This situation is comparable to a community that is occupied by a foreign army.

As a result of this community occupancy, the citizens in their agitated and emotional state begin to act out their frustrations. They are not able to recognize that the aggravation is coming from the police so they lash out at each other by committing crimes that they wouldn't ordinarily commit. When human beings are forced to live together in unfavorable conditions such as poverty, overcrowding, lack of quality education, lack of employment, racism, and coupled with being "over policed," historically their crime rate increases and remains high.

**Table 1. Inmates, by race, age, and number of sentences ever served**

| | | Number of sentences ever served | | | | | |
|---|---|---|---|---|---|---|---|
| Race and age | Total | None | One | Two | Three | Four | Five or more |
| All races[1] | 191,367 | 494 | 55,772 | 43,907 | 36,060 | 23,773 | 31,360 |
| Under 20 | 15,817 | 138 | 6,511 | 4,193 | 2,824 | 1,227 | 924 |
| 20 | 9,275 | 19 | 3,515 | 2,309 | 1,848 | 963 | 621 |
| 21 | 11,677 | 0 | 4,303 | 2,835 | 2,123 | 1,225 | 1,191 |
| 22 | 11,733 | 22 | 4,058 | 3,009 | 2,277 | 1,122 | 1,245 |
| 23 | 12,842 | 61 | 4,103 | 3,563 | 2,477 | 1,328 | 1,308 |

| Race and age | Total | None | One | Two | Three | Four | Five or more |
|---|---|---|---|---|---|---|---|
| | Number of sentences ever served | | | | | | |
| 24 | 11,654 | 19 | 3,820 | 2,732 | 2,554 | 1,335 | 1,194 |
| 25 | 11,246 | 87 | 3,360 | 3,013 | 1,905 | 1,438 | 1,443 |
| 26 | 10,498 | 21 | 3,095 | 2,628 | 2,022 | 1,269 | 1,484 |
| 27 | 8,326 | 21 | 2,455 | 1,794 | 1,472 | 1,091 | 1,493 |
| 28 | 7,226 | 0 | 2,076 | 1,544 | 1,304 | 962 | 1,341 |
| 29 | 7,600 | 0 | 1,823 | 1,668 | 1,468 | 1,037 | 1,604 |
| 30-34 | 27,128 | 0 | 5,734 | 5,648 | 5,384 | 4,388 | 5,975 |
| 35-39 | 16,280 | 20 | 3,478 | 3,102 | 3,250 | 3,396 | 4,033 |
| 40-44 | 11,486 | 20 | 2,442 | 2,522 | 2,148 | 1,446 | 2,907 |
| 45-49 | 8,096 | 22 | 2,136 | 1,334 | 1,381 | 1,092 | 2,131 |
| 50 and over | 10,440 | 42 | 2,841 | 2,014 | 1,603 | 1,454 | 2,488 |
| Not reported | 43 | 0 | 21 | 0 | 22 | 0 | 0 |
| Median age | 27.1 | 24.3 | 25.5 | 26.1 | 27.0 | 28.9 | 31.6 |
| White | 97,658 | 305 | 27,133 | 21,325 | 18,572 | 11,837 | 18,485 |
| Under 20 | 7,413 | 59 | 2,956 | 1,997 | 1,272 | 636 | 492 |
| 20 | 4,762 | 19 | 1,810 | 1,201 | 931 | 449 | 352 |
| 21 | 5,044 | 0 | 1,977 | 1,220 | 1,168 | 458 | 682 |
| 22 | 5,657 | 0 | 1,667 | 1,402 | 1,116 | 659 | 813 |
| 23 | 6,057 | 61 | 1,778 | 1,620 | 1,228 | 632 | 738 |
| 24 | 5,408 | 19 | 1,405 | 1,236 | 1,347 | 689 | 711 |
| 25 | 4,876 | 42 | 1,219 | 1,220 | 853 | 729 | 813 |
| 26 | 5,199 | 21 | 1,396 | 1,194 | 1,070 | 652 | 866 |
| 27 | 3,934 | 21 | 1,210 | 707 | 811 | 515 | 670 |
| 28 | 3,431 | 0 | 937 | 665 | 435 | 517 | 877 |
| 29 | 4,301 | 0 | 1,158 | 946 | 802 | 506 | 888 |
| 30-34 | 14,471 | 0 | 2,994 | 2,965 | 2,988 | 2,017 | 3,507 |
| 35-39 | 9,372 | 20 | 2,047 | 1,622 | 1,807 | 1,270 | 2,606 |
| 40-44 | 6,620 | 20 | 1,553 | 1,505 | 1,109 | 804 | 1,629 |
| 45-49 | 4,419 | 0 | 1,316 | 722 | 673 | 402 | 1,305 |
| 50 and over | 6,213 | 20 | 1,710 | 1,104 | 939 | 904 | 1,535 |
| Not reported | 22 | 0 | 0 | 0 | 22 | 0 | 0 |
| Median age | 28.0 | 24.7 | 26.5 | 26.6 | 27.4 | 29.0 | 31.9 |
| Black | 89,747 | 149 | 27,894 | 21,712 | 16,728 | 11,172 | 12,093 |
| Under 20 | 8,139 | 39 | 3,433 | 2,156 | 1,532 | 548 | 431 |
| 20 | 4,323 | 0 | 1,705 | 1,086 | 827 | 476 | 229 |
| 21 | 5,945 | 0 | 2,306 | 1,584 | 892 | 704 | 469 |
| 22 | 5,816 | 22 | 2,330 | 1,567 | 1,085 | 442 | 371 |
| 23 | 6,494 | 0 | 2,284 | 1,857 | 1,228 | 636 | 489 |
| 24 | 5,984 | 0 | 2,357 | 1,413 | 1,147 | 624 | 443 |
| 25 | 6,093 | 45 | 2,037 | 1,684 | 1,009 | 709 | 609 |
| 26 | 5,169 | 0 | 1,656 | 1,434 | 887 | 617 | 575 |
| 27 | 4,259 | 0 | 1,245 | 1,045 | 615 | 532 | 823 |
| 28 | 3,575 | 0 | 1,119 | 770 | 845 | 423 | 418 |
| 29 | 3,152 | 0 | 642 | 721 | 622 | 470 | 696 |
| 30-34 | 12,056 | 0 | 2,699 | 2,552 | 2,333 | 2,156 | 2,316 |
| 35-39 | 6,470 | 0 | 1,366 | 1,392 | 1,379 | 1,059 | 1,273 |
| 40-44 | 4,638 | 0 | 871 | 998 | 995 | 580 | 1,194 |
| 45-49 | 3,573 | 22 | 777 | 571 | 708 | 669 | 826 |
| 50 and over | 4,041 | 21 | 1,646 | 891 | 623 | 527 | 933 |

| Race and age | Total | None | One | Two | Three | Four | Five or more |
|---|---|---|---|---|---|---|---|
| Not reported ...... | 21 | 0 | 21 | 0 | 0 | 0 | 0 |
| Median age ....... | 26.4 | 25.3 | 24.8 | 25.7 | 26.7 | 28.7 | 31.1 |

NOTE: Detail may not add to total shown because of rounding. Values under 300 are based on too few sample cases to be statistically reliable.
[1]Includes inmates of races other than white or black, as well as those whose race was not reported.

Statistics taken from: PROFILE OF STATE PRISON INMATES; SOCIODEMOGRAPHIC FINDINGS FROM THE 1974 SURVEY OF INMATES OF STATE CORRECTIONAL FACILITIES. U.S. DEPT. OF JUSTICE LEAA, A NATIONAL PRISONERS STATISTICS SPECIAL REPORT.

## Table 2. Sentenced inmates, by offense and race

| Offense | All races[1] | White | Black | Other |
|---|---|---|---|---|
| Total ---------------------------- | 187,487 | 95,000 | 88,628 | 3,272 |
| Violent offenses ---------------------- | 97,523 | 40,916 | 54,526 | 1,728 |
| Homicide ------------------------- | 33,958 | 14,708 | 18,524 | 584 |
| Murder or attempted murder -------- | 25,841 | 11,583 | 13,691 | 444 |
| Murder ---------------------- | 21,400 | 9,836 | 11,124 | 338 |
| Attempted murder -------------- | 4,441 | 1,747 | 2,567 | 107 |
| Manslaughter -------------------- | 8,117 | 3,125 | 4,833 | 140 |
| Kidnaping ------------------------ | 2,315 | 1,640 | 614 | 41 |
| Sexual assault --------------------- | 9,870 | 4,702 | 5,006 | 142 |
| Rape ------------------------- | 8,514 | 3,708 | 4,664 | 142 |
| Statutory rape -------------------- | 619 | 383 | 236 | 0 |
| Lewd act with child --------------- | 529 | 489 | 40 | 0 |
| Other --------------------------- | 208 | 122 | 65 | 0 |
| Robbery ------------------------- | 42,294 | 15,428 | 26,181 | 513 |
| Armed robbery -------------------- | 28,746 | 10,878 | 17,390 | 348 |
| Unarmed robbery ----------------- | 5,904 | 1,908 | 3,894 | 103 |
| Undetermined -------------------- | 7,644 | 2,642 | 4,898 | 63 |
| Assault ------------------------- | 9,084 | 4,437 | 4,200 | 447 |
| Aggravated assault --------------- | 5,723 | 2,794 | 2,718 | 212 |
| Simple assault -------------------- | 1,691 | 783 | 735 | 173 |
| Undetermined -------------------- | 1,670 | 860 | 747 | 62 |
| Property offenses ---------------------- | 61,489 | 36,976 | 23,280 | 1,082 |
| Burglary ------------------------ | 34,025 | 20,261 | 13,129 | 554 |
| Larceny or auto theft --------------- | 16,252 | 9,198 | 6,628 | 403 |
| Larceny ------------------------ | 12,316 | 6,509 | 5,486 | 321 |
| Auto theft --------------------- | 3,935 | 2,689 | 1,142 | 81 |
| Other --------------------------- | 11,213 | 7,517 | 3,523 | 125 |
| Forgery, fraud, or embezzlement ..... | 8,167 | 5,549 | 2,555 | 41 |
| Arson ------------------------- | 1,017 | 717 | 277 | 22 |
| Stolen property offense ----------- | 1,950 | 1,192 | 670 | 62 |
| Property damage ------------------ | 80 | 59 | 21 | 0 |

| Offense | All races[1] | White | Black | Other |
|---|---|---|---|---|
| Drug offenses | 18,807 | 10,992 | 7,605 | 148 |
| Major (all offenses except possession and marijuana | 8,131 | 4,919 | 3,147 | 63 |
| Heroin | 2,773 | 1,263 | 1,509 | 0 |
| Other drug except marijuana | 5,358 | 3,656 | 1,638 | 63 |
| Minor (possession and all marijuana offenses) | 10,676 | 6,072 | 4,457 | 85 |
| Marijuana except possession | 1,861 | 1,538 | 302 | 0 |
| Heroin possession | 2,651 | 1,233 | 1,377 | 20 |
| Other drug possession | 1,159 | 793 | 345 | 21 |
| Unknown drug possession | 2,050 | 1,050 | 980 | 20 |
| Marijuana possession | 1,142 | 792 | 327 | 23 |
| Activity unknown | 1,813 | 666 | 1,126 | 0 |
| Public order offenses | 9,669 | 6,116 | 3,217 | 314 |
| Weapons offense | 1,857 | 647 | 1,165 | 46 |
| Other sex offense | 2,117 | 1,720 | 376 | 21 |
| Drunk driving | 1,130 | 735 | 325 | 70 |
| Flight or escape | 984 | 791 | 105 | 88 |
| Habitual criminal | 146 | 106 | 40 | 0 |
| Jail offense | 3,413 | 2,094 | 1,208 | 89 |
| Other | 22 | 22 | 0 | 0 |

NOTE: Detail may not add to total shown because of rounding. Values under 300 are based on too few sample cases to be statistically reliable.
[1]Includes inmates whose race was not reported.

Statistics taken from: PROFILE OF STATE PRISON INMATES; SOCIODEMOGRAPHIC FINDINGS FROM THE 1974 SURVEY OF INMATES OF STATE CORRECTIONAL FACILITIES.

U.S. DEPT. OF JUSTICE LEAA, A NATIONAL PRISONERS STATISTICS SPECIAL REPORT.

## Table 3. Sentenced inmates, by race, offense, and age at admission

| Race and offense | Total | Under 20 | 20 | 21 | 22 | 23 | 24 | 25-29 | 30-34 | 35-39 | 40 and over | Not reported | Median age |
|---|---|---|---|---|---|---|---|---|---|---|---|---|---|
| All races[1] | 187,487 | 33,575 | 14,498 | 12,629 | 13,157 | 12,201 | 10,054 | 36,401 | 20,394 | 12,802 | 20,268 | 1,507 | 24.7 |
| Violent offenses | 97,523 | 17,310 | 7,728 | 6,309 | 6,877 | 6,241 | 5,466 | 19,375 | 10,683 | 6,840 | 9,859 | 835 | 24.7 |
| Murder or attempted murder | 25,841 | 4,032 | 1,390 | 1,461 | 1,473 | 1,304 | 1,501 | 4,778 | 2,967 | 2,093 | 4,543 | 317 | 26.2 |
| Manslaughter | 8,117 | 842 | 434 | 276 | 420 | 336 | 354 | 1,705 | 976 | 775 | 1,936 | 65 | 28.9 |
| Rape | 9,133 | 1,646 | 798 | 689 | 453 | 639 | 441 | 2,129 | 1,062 | 655 | 601 | 21 | 24.8 |
| Robbery | 42,294 | 9,037 | 4,170 | 3,247 | 3,633 | 3,180 | 2,613 | 8,115 | 4,189 | 2,254 | 1,508 | 349 | 23.3 |
| Assault | 9,084 | 1,472 | 694 | 522 | 754 | 660 | 367 | 1,857 | 1,077 | 774 | 847 | 62 | 25.1 |
| Other | 3,052 | 292 | 244 | 123 | 144 | 122 | 190 | 791 | 412 | 288 | 424 | 21 | 27.6 |
| Property offenses | 61,489 | 13,080 | 5,109 | 4,381 | 4,301 | 3,932 | 2,939 | 11,428 | 5,916 | 3,984 | 5,904 | 516 | 23.9 |
| Burglary | 34,895 | 7,711 | 2,988 | 2,647 | 2,620 | 2,358 | 1,675 | 5,969 | 3,175 | 1,952 | 2,564 | 366 | 23.4 |
| Larceny or auto theft | 16,252 | 4,186 | 1,471 | 1,000 | 1,050 | 923 | 761 | 2,662 | 1,296 | 974 | 1,719 | 128 | 23.3 |
| Other | 11,213 | 1,202 | 649 | 614 | 631 | 652 | 503 | 2,797 | 1,444 | 1,058 | 1,619 | 22 | 27.1 |
| Drug or public order offenses | 28,475 | 3,185 | 1,460 | 1,940 | 1,979 | 2,027 | 1,649 | 5,597 | 3,795 | 1,979 | 4,506 | 157 | 26.3 |
| Drug | 18,807 | 1,745 | 1,350 | 1,581 | 1,616 | 1,389 | 1,272 | 3,977 | 2,483 | 1,269 | 2,067 | 55 | 25.4 |
| Public order | 9,669 | 1,440 | 310 | 358 | 363 | 638 | 377 | 1,620 | 1,312 | 709 | 2,439 | 102 | 29.3 |
| White | 95,000 | 15,133 | 6,924 | 6,449 | 6,250 | 5,767 | 4,937 | 18,556 | 11,004 | 7,460 | 11,710 | 770 | 25.3 |
| Violent offenses | 40,916 | 5,562 | 2,882 | 2,410 | 2,468 | 2,401 | 2,210 | 8,682 | 5,323 | 3,868 | 4,757 | 353 | 26.1 |
| Murder or attempted murder | 11,583 | 1,624 | 494 | 573 | 601 | 572 | 671 | 2,003 | 1,388 | 1,172 | 2,297 | 129 | 27.4 |
| Manslaughter | 3,125 | 267 | 160 | 63 | 190 | 83 | 146 | 836 | 412 | 312 | 633 | 23 | 29.1 |
| Rape | 4,091 | 438 | 386 | 341 | 186 | 165 | 168 | 1,239 | 402 | 322 | 284 | 0 | 26.0 |
| Robbery | 15,426 | 2,478 | 1,385 | 1,104 | 948 | 1,054 | 931 | 3,038 | 2,014 | 1,425 | 891 | 139 | 24.7 |
| Assault | 4,437 | 580 | 314 | 289 | 460 | 486 | 166 | 860 | 557 | 389 | 357 | 42 | 24.8 |
| Other | 2,262 | 185 | 142 | 42 | 188 | 103 | 129 | 647 | 351 | 249 | 300 | 21 | 28.2 |
| Property offenses | 14,976 | 7,620 | 2,891 | 2,694 | 2,286 | 2,141 | 1,755 | 6,558 | 3,691 | 2,758 | 4,279 | 323 | 24.4 |
| Burglary | 20,261 | 4,363 | 1,857 | 1,694 | 1,437 | 1,354 | 1,076 | 3,301 | 1,751 | 1,305 | 1,690 | 281 | 23.5 |
| Larceny or auto theft | 9,194 | 2,514 | 641 | 619 | 433 | 371 | 401 | 1,406 | 954 | 658 | 1,180 | 20 | 24.0 |
| Other | 7,517 | 759 | 383 | 421 | 419 | 416 | 277 | 1,649 | 986 | 774 | 1,407 | 22 | 27.9 |
| Drug or public order offenses | 17,107 | 1,951 | 1,152 | 1,345 | 1,498 | 1,245 | 972 | 3,316 | 2,010 | 855 | 2,674 | 94 | 25.4 |
| Drug | 10,992 | 1,104 | 989 | 1,201 | 1,241 | 887 | 740 | 2,302 | 1,124 | 405 | 944 | 55 | 24.1 |
| Public order | 6,116 | 847 | 153 | 144 | 251 | 357 | 232 | 1,015 | 886 | 451 | 1,730 | 39 | 30.2 |

**Age at admission**

| Race and offense | Total | Under 20 | 20 | 21 | 22 | 23 | 24 | 25-29 | 30-34 | 35-39 | 40 and over | Not reported | Median age |
|---|---|---|---|---|---|---|---|---|---|---|---|---|---|
| Black -------------- | 68,628 | 17,906 | 7,373 | 5,780 | 6,704 | 6,096 | 4,952 | 16,960 | 8,961 | 5,020 | 8,182 | 695 | 24.0 |
| Violent offenses ------- | 54,526 | 11,362 | 4,769 | 3,774 | 4,328 | 3,742 | 3,153 | 10,225 | 5,100 | 2,761 | 4,873 | 440 | 23.8 |
| Murder or attempted murder ------- | 13,691 | 2,359 | 986 | 815 | 873 | 711 | 809 | 2,499 | 1,538 | 878 | 2,144 | 167 | 25.4 |
| Manslaughter ------- | 4,833 | 556 | 273 | 213 | 211 | 234 | 189 | 848 | 542 | 463 | 1,261 | 42 | 28.8 |
| Rape ------- | 4,900 | 1,177 | 411 | 329 | 287 | 478 | 273 | 850 | 439 | 334 | 326 | 0 | 23.5 |
| Robbery ------- | 26,181 | 6,373 | 2,747 | 2,123 | 2,625 | 2,086 | 1,620 | 4,951 | 2,108 | 767 | 571 | 210 | 22.7 |
| Assault ------- | 4,200 | 810 | 360 | 210 | 271 | 218 | 201 | 952 | 410 | 280 | 467 | 20 | 25.1 |
| Other ------- | 720 | 86 | 82 | 82 | 61 | 19 | 61 | 124 | 62 | 39 | 104 | 0 | 24.5 |
| Property offenses ------- | 23,280 | 5,352 | 2,116 | 1,522 | 1,931 | 1,592 | 1,142 | 4,592 | 2,184 | 1,159 | 1,498 | 193 | 23.4 |
| Burglary ------- | 13,129 | 3,319 | 1,092 | 931 | 1,145 | 852 | 556 | 2,334 | 1,404 | 603 | 809 | 85 | 23.0 |
| Larceny or auto theft ------- | 6,528 | 1,610 | 768 | 399 | 573 | 526 | 360 | 1,150 | 343 | 294 | 498 | 108 | 22.8 |
| Other ------- | 3,523 | 423 | 257 | 193 | 212 | 214 | 226 | 1,107 | 437 | 262 | 193 | 0 | 25.7 |
| Drug or public order offenses ------- | 10,822 | 1,192 | 487 | 484 | 446 | 762 | 657 | 2,144 | 1,677 | 1,100 | 1,810 | 62 | 28.0 |
| Drug ------- | 7,865 | 620 | 361 | 381 | 334 | 481 | 512 | 1,652 | 1,296 | 865 | 1,103 | 0 | 27.9 |
| Public order ------- | 3,217 | 572 | 125 | 103 | 112 | 281 | 145 | 491 | 381 | 235 | 708 | 62 | 28.2 |

NOTE: Detail may not add to total shown because of rounding. Values under 300 are based on too few sample cases to be statistically reliable.
[1]Includes inmates of races other than white or black, as well as those whose race was not reported.

Statistics taken from: PROFILE OF STATE PRISON INMATES; SOCIODEMOGRAPHIC FINDINGS FROM THE 1974 SURVEY OF INMATES OF STATE CORRECTIONAL FACILITIES. U.S. DEPT. OF JUSTICE LEAA, A NATIONAL PRISONERS STATISTICS SPECIAL REPORT.

Crime, and conditions that perpetuate crime, has historically been directed against the poor. This is the scheme of criminal conspirators who still seek to dominate the world. When a man is found guilty of a crime, he may be indicted for that crime as well as other short-comings. He is indicted because of his own ignorance by those who seek to control him. Examine the moral condition of America, and you will find that it has retrogressed. It has grown progressively weaker through the designs of Satan.

Imam Warith Deen Muhammad recently stated, "I remember a time when dope was primarily a problem for Bilalians, but it didn't take too long to spread. We've been the victims of dope for 20 years —the only victims of dope. But, all of a sudden, we find Mexicans the victims of dope, Caucasians the victims of dope, even the very members of the elite class, their sons, their daughters, the victims of dope". (Source: Bilalian News—**Humanity Is One,** July 27, 1979, pp. 16-17).

The weakness in society will spread. Racism and ignorance will keep human beings segregated (separated). While some are spreading evil or giving it the freedom to grow in certain sections, eventually this evil will creep in like a poisonous snake and sift into the nose of those whom we have been trying to protect. Hence, we have crime as an epidemic in America.

# Part II
## Miseducation of the Masses

This criminal act of miseducation (denying the masses proper education) is perpetrated against the poor who are, subsequently, robbed of their human strength before birth.

What is a proper education? A proper education is one that is designed to allow its recipient to enter into the mainstream of his or her society without undue hinderance or stress. This is the kind of education that will allow one to become productive and not just relegated to the role of consumer. A proper education will allow the individual as well as his group to become a political force as well as an economical force that is on a par (equal) with that of all other peoples within that given society.

Examine how America's public educational system at the elementary level concentrates its efforts on influencing the citizenship beliefs and values of its students. It has been suggested by some studies that: 1) compliance to rules and authority is the major focus of education in elementary schools, and compliance is encouraged through force or threat of force; 2) the citizen's right to participate in government is under-emphasized in the school's curriculum; 3) the role of political parties and partisanship receives less attention in the elementary school than any other topic. (Source: Robert Hess and Judith V. Torney. The Development of Basic Attitudes and Values Toward Government and Citizenship During the Elementary School Years, Part I; Chicago: University of Chicago, Cooperative Research Project No. 1078, 1965).

The school is justifiably used to promote loyalty, orientations toward governmental figures and institutions, attitudes toward citizens' duties, and conceptions of citizens' rights and powers. The socialization of loyalty to the nation is reinforced through formal classroom rituals, (e.g., displaying the American flag, pledging allegiance to the flag, and singing patriotic songs). Why aren't the masses educated by the public schools to feel strongly that they too have a right to participate in government?

The school curriculum generally ignores the unpleasant and ugly aspects of political life in the United States, as it emphasizes ideal norms and myths about government responsiveness to the demands of the average citizen. For example, the curriculum in our public schools ignores the extremely high unemployment rate, especially

41

as it affects the minorities. Nor does the curriculum address the problems of political impotence with reference to the common people, and the serious problem of racism is never properly addressed with a view to resolving it. We have only to look at the recent mayoral campaign in Chicago in order to get a realistic view of racism in America. Even though Congressman Washington won the mayoral election, racism too had its victory. In summary, the curriculum as it stands continues to neglect emphasizing the need to achieve in the basic areas of politics, economics, education and cultural development. The unrealistic image that the curriculum presents about American social and political life is confirmed by investigations of civics and social studies textbooks. This kind of curriculum does a disservice to the American child (the future voter), because it gives him a distorted view of his capability.

Great harm is done to the child when he is taught that freedom or democracy really exist when, in fact, it does not. The average adult in America does not know what freedom and democracy really mean. This exaggerated feeling of one's capability to influence the system can bring about a deep feeling of frustration and bitterness. This kind of gross hypocrisy cannot be reconciled by the masses. Many members of this class are driven to crime out of sheer frustration and ignorance. It has been demonstrated that the average child is not given the opportunity to move progressively through lower levels of involvement (attachment to the nation) to more assertive and direct forms of participation in the operation of the political system.

The masses of poor children are not considered "average". So, what chance do they have of enjoying the American "good life" of freedom and democracy? Our public schools should be used to educate our children and not miseducate them. The seriousness of crime, corrupt governmental practices, price fixing, crimes against environment, etc., should be taught from kindergarten through college. The seamy side of our society has to be dealt with openly. If it is not, we are actually covering up criminal acts against our country, our society and the citizens. It is easy for a poor person to justify committing crimes if he uses the same value system as our government, "the survival of the fittest".

# CHAPTER 6
# CAUSATION OF CRIME AMONG THE POOR

There have been many theories offered by psychologists, sociologists, criminologists and others, to explain the causation of crime. But, there has been no general agreement on any theory.

The American Muslim Mission has learned the basic cause of crime. Under the leadership of Imam Warith Deen Muhammad and his profound teachings, we have been blessed by Almighty God (Allah) to discover the very root of crime.

When one speaks of crime and the criminal, one should use the concept of a criminal mentality. This will afford one a better opportunity to identify the criminal and, hence, the **cause of crime.** It is the mind, the mental state or mentality that produces the criminal act. Or, to be more concise, it is that mentality that produced the act that has been labeled and legislated as being criminal.

When the accused has been tried and convicted legally, has anything been done to correct that mentality which produced the act? If the criminal is executed by hanging, electrocution, gas chamber, etc., will the mentality or the mind be executed along with the man? You may say, "Well, at least we don't have to worry about him". This is true, but now we have to worry about you and everyone else. Why? Because the same mentality that produced the executed criminal is still alive in our society today.

We have properly diagnosed the cause of the disease of criminal behavior as being in the minds of the people as well as in the mind of Western society. "There has been an unnatural, grafted mentality of Caucasion leadership that has brought about big problems for people of color the world over and for Caucasions themselves." Something that has been grafted is not original. For example, if you graft a lemon tree onto an orange tree, you will get a cross between the two which would result in the grapefruit.

The causation of crime occurs the moment truth is withheld from the people. This hiding of truth causes the people to form a false concept of reality. The problem is seeing the world in false pictures. In our society, a picture has already been designed for you to look at before you become acquainted with the object. Imam Warith Deem Muhammad stated that, "Before you come to know what a woman is for yourself, this society has already given you a false picture of women. It has also given you a false picture of man, child, mother and everything else. Before you get old enough to see things in the world for yourself, they have given you a false picture so that when you get old enough, you won't be able to see the reality of things."

43

The average inmate in America's penitentiary has not been prepared to live in this world. The simple knowledge that the world has to offer the people to enable them to make some social progress has been denied to the Bilalian people. People of color could not go to school and get the same knowledge that Caucasian rulers got. We know that a disproportionate percentage of inmates in America are Bilalians. This is no accident, it is by design.

The physical form does not dominate the world, minds rule the world. These ruling minds know that as long as they are able to keep you thinking on a physical level, you are not going to cause them trouble. If you do cause any trouble, they will be able to effectively deal with it. That is, provided you remain a physical, non-thinking individual.

People do not know the definition of man unless they have learned it since Imam Warith Deen Muhammad has been teaching. Man means mind and this mind is composed of words. What is a word? A word is anything that delivers a message to the mind. Now that you have taken on new knowledge, you should be able to understand the causation of crime. Crime is caused simply by manipulating the minds of the people.

We use the Bilalian (Black) American as the classic example because he is the world's witness (a people enslaved by mind control). He is the classic guinea pig and has been for a long time. Their minds have been so thoroughly misshapened that they could easily be classified as dead. In Medical science it is said that if your brain dies, you may be considered legally dead. When you look at the Bilalian people, their behavior, their reality concepts, their capacity to make rational decisions, can they truthfully be diagnosed as living?

Mind manipulation is the cause of corruption in all societies. For example, look at the clothing styles and dress habits that have been forced on the public in America. The mind has to first be prepared before a male will wear four and five inch heels on his shoes. Unisex clothing is a classic form of mind manipulation. It is this diabolical practice that has robbed man of his human dignity and self-respect. This criminal behavior is the same technique that was used during the time of that great prophet, Jesus. Jesus and the prophets before him had their true messages corrupted and twisted so badly, that by the time the messages reached the masses, it confused them. The mind of the masses were locked up in symbolic language of truth mixed up with falsehood. Prophet Moses, in the Book of Exodus (Bible) had to constantly struggle with the people he led in order to prevent distortions of God's message. As soon as he would leave the people for a brief stay, they would distort the truth he spoke and twist it to fit their corrupt aims and desires.

The masses have been fed false knowledge by the satanic minded corrupters of religion. Therefore, this society must contend with a Criminal Justice System that has enough manpower, real estate, and financial wealth to compete with the City of Chicago. The mentality that produces criminals has also produced the mechanism by which he can control them. Remember, as long as man remains physical in his thinking, he will be dominated by the minds that molded him. When a man has been made to think all physical, all one has to do is feed his physical lusts and his aberrated or inflated appetites, and he will remain a slave of Satan.

Satan has studied the nature of man. He knows man's passions, drives and inclinations. When the opportunity presents itself, satan will begin to feed man's passions and heighten his drives. He knows that there is a part of man's nature, which we mentioned earlier, that is inclined to disobey, i.e., refuse to accept truth and reality. Satan also knows the powerful influence of materialism. He is the beast that is spoken of so often in the Bible.

When man's passions and drives are dominated by materialism, satan begins to reinforce this urge for domination and the seeds of crime have been sown. Satan has a mentality that seeks dominance over the world's masses. People have been prepared to accept arrogant domination because of selfish materialistic greed. The society is now ripe for an ongoing criminal epidemic.

Western society does not have a law against practising crime. It is alright to practise crime in America unless you are caught. Crime is encouraged in America. For example, if access to correct knowledge is denied to the masses, they will fall into the many traps of materialism. They have been programmed to satisfy their biological drives and their lust for materialism at the risk of losing human dignity and physical freedom. This could be classified as rape, robbery, fraud and theft of the human essence.

The masses in America have not been taught to use logic. They have not been trained to think rationally, to move intelligently and with circumspect. The opinion of the masses can be swayed as easily as dust is blown about by the wind. For example, the controversy about human sexuality has been presented to the public through the media by those who subtly seek the public's approval. The shrewd satanic conspirators know that the public (the masses) can be convinced that homosexuality is normal and poses no great threat to society.

There are an estimated 20 million homosexual men and women

45

in America according to a recent article in the April 14, 1980 issue of **U.S. News and World Report** magazine. The article also indicates that although open advocacy of homosexual interests is carried out by only a small number, evidence of rising public tolerance and approval is growing. In 1974, the American Psychiatric Association removed homosexuality from its list of mental illnesses, specifying instead a "sexual-orientation disorder" that referred only to those who were unhappy with their same sex orientation. In 1979, the U.S. Surgeon General declared that homosexuality by itself would no longer be considered a "mental disease or defect".

Upon examining the logic, or lack of logic, in the moves made by the American Psychiatric Association and the U.S. Surgeon General, one must conclude that there is no logic. It is illogical to say that homosexuality is not a mental illness, but that it is a "sexual-orientation disorder". This kind of language is confusing, and it clearly demonstrates that the American Psychiatric Association is incapable of making logical and rational decisions. According to the dictionary's definition, disorder means: 1) lack of order or regular arrangement, disarrangement, confusion; 2) a derangement of physical or mental health; or 3) a breach of order, a public disturbance. Therefore, by definition, a man (mind) in a male body that seeks to function as a female has a mental problem. This problem may be referred to as a mental illness or a mental disorder. Both terms mean basically the same thing. This confusing language is designed for the masses. When a large body of intellectuals, who deal primarily with the mind, openly declare that homosexuality is not a mental illness, but a "sexual-orientation disorder", the public normally will accept its findings. A morally weak society will readily accept justification for weakness because it has been mentally prepared to do so.

The office of the United States Surgeon General is a high office in our Government and as such, it should be respected. This office has great influence on the public: an example being the effectiveness of its stand on smoking. It has impacted the amount of tobacco used in America. Therefore, its announcement indicating that homosexuality is not a mental illness will be looked upon with some credibility by the masses because, as we have shown, they have not been prepared to think logically.

The public has been taught that the flesh is sinful, that it is inclined to commit immoral acts, and, one has no control over it. Christian doctrine bears this out. The public should be taught that it is the mind that should motivate the flesh. The flesh should not motivate the mind (man). The flesh will respond normally to its

46

physical environment without deviation. It is the mind that directs the body. With the exception of physical reflexes, the body can only respond to thought processes of the mind.

For example, if the male or female mind of the homosexual does not "see" a physical attraction, it will not respond. Man's physical body never becomes sexually aroused or attracted until after the mind has first been aroused. Therefore, the conclusion of the U.S. Surgeon General was not a logical conclusion. But, the public will generally accept his views as mentioned previously.

This kind of misguidance by responsible organizations and office holders is criminal; i.e., it robs the people of their common sense and keeps them sedated to the realities of creation and humanity in particular. This misinformation will steer many members of our society into criminal activities that they would not normally consider. For example, the type of clothing that is being designed for young men today suggests that they display their sex organs and buttocks through tight fitting pants. A homosexual may be attracted to the young man wearing such apparel. This homosexual would approach his "victim" with some pretty strong arguments.

First, the U.S. Surgeon General said it was perfectly normal and secondly the American Psychiatric Association also stated that "my desire to commit sodomy is not a sign of mental illness". Homosexuality is just one example of many growing problems that have been produced and supported by denying the public correct knowledge.

Another problem that is prominent is the aberrated buying habits of the public. The rate of persons filing bankruptcy has increased by 200 percent in some areas of America. We are having serious problems coping with inflation and our public educational system is on the verge of collapse.

The masses of people (the public) have been given the approval by their leadership to engage in any kind of social activity that will satisfy them. This moral degeneracy has appealed to the public and the public has accepted the appeal. Robbery, rape and other offenses are encouraged so long as the perpetrator gets a "good feeling" during or after the commission of his crime. The leadership in America has condoned any act by its citizens so long as they do not get caught.

The Criminal Justice System must direct its research and development efforts toward understanding how and why crime is perpetuated among the masses. Statistics cited in this book and in many others consistently point to the reality that crime is purposely promoted.

# CHAPTER 7

# HUMAN BEHAVIOR AS IT RELATES
# TO CORRECTIONS

Corrections by implication is a discipline that is directed toward altering human behavior. Yet, the study of human behavior has been one of the most neglected areas in this field. More efforts are directed towards the mechanics of operating the institutions rather than towards understanding human behavior. Correctional officers cannot apply the same "common sense" principles in the treatment of inmates that they learned during their own psychological and social development. The correctional officer's "common sense" supplies him with limited stereotypical beliefs or majority judgments. For example, a Caucasian officer may think that most Bilalian (Black) inmates that come from urban areas belong to some gang, that all Bilalian inmates have a strong hatred for Caucasian guards, or that they will steal and cannot be trusted.

The modern correctional officer cannot afford to base his decisions on what are usually termed "common sense notions". These notions usually lead to erroneous assumptions and decisions. The correctional officer must first be taught to use his five common senses rationally and morally. Prophet Muhammad (P.B.U.H.) taught that man must use his five senses or his five senses would deprive him. These senses must be used to make rational decisions based on moral strength. That is, is it right and just? Common sense notions based on prejudices often circumvent the truth. The purpose of education is to increase one's capacity to solve problems. Therefore, an accurate study of human behavior will enable the correctional officer to learn general principles of human behavior that will help him solve daily problems and aid in reforming the inmate.

Before one can understand others, he must first understand himself. When one understands oneself, his objectivity is increased. This, in turn, reduces a number of prejudicial factors that this society has made inherent in the performance of correctional duties. As we have indicated in a previous Chapter, the human being must be guided by Allah (God) through His prophets, in order that he may know himself because his intellect is far too limited. College training and correctional training is done within the confines of one's personal family, community and social reality concepts. One's personality determines how one will use the formal training that he acquires.

Even though a person spends years in college and perhaps

months in correctional training, he eventually will become a correctional officer whose attitudes and behavior will reflect the personality of his community. This personality will, in turn, determine his performance. Remember, the formal learning institutions are products of the environment.

Under the teachings of Al-Islam, the inmate must be encouraged to understand that this world's reality concepts are false. Because of this "artificial reality", the Bilalian people in particular are operating with artificial brains. The problem also applies to the correctional administration and officers.

"The grafted (unnatural) mentality of Caucasian leadership has created a problem for people of color the world over and for Caucasians themselves. The problem is seeing the world in false pictures. A picture has already been designed for you to see before you even become acquainted with the object. Before you come to know what a woman is for yourself, this society has already given you a false picture of man, child, father, mother and everything else. Before you get old enough to see things in the world for yourself, they have given you a false picture so that when you get old enough, you won't be able to see the reality of things." (Source: Warith Deen Muhammad: Lectures of Imam W.D. Muhammad. W.D. Muhammad Publications, Inc., 1978, p. 8). This quote from Imam Muhammad goes directly to the heart and exposes the root of many problems. The inmate, upon hearing these truths, is galvanized to think and think deeply?

If you have a false image of yourself and everything else in creation, you are a slave to the mentality that gave you this false world. This is a world of darkness and ignorance to the masses of people. The inmates begin to realize that they have had very little choice in how they would conduct their lives. This world has already plotted your course prior to your existence. When the inmate learns that man means mind, that man is a thinking being, that the body will not respond without first getting a message from the brain, he must raise the question: "How can you think for yourself when your thinking apparatus has been supplanted or clocked to think and respond like a computer?"

At this point, let us cite a few obvious examples of how people have been programmed with artificial brains. The use of alcohol and tobacco cost the consumer and society billions of dollars in loss of productive man hours, medical costs, financial loss to the individual families, etc. An account of the human misery and suffering produced by these two products alone would fill volumes upon volumes. Yet, we do not have the mind strength to rid our society of these evils. This is a classic example of total lack of self control or mental discipline.

Youth gangs are on the rise again and they are far worse than they used to be. This increase poses a serious setback for sociologists and policemen who have worked for years to defuse juvenile violence. According to Detective Sergeant Vernon J. Geberth of New York's South Bronx area: "These groups are loosely knit associations of street kids whose actions are completely unpredictable and prone to the worst kind of violence." (Source: U.S. News and World Report —August 20, 1979, pp. 46 Youth Gangs: They're Back—Growing Worse.)

A recent study indicates that nearly half the violent street crimes in the nation's 1,000 cities with populations over 25,000 are committed by youth groups and the number is climbing. This study was headed by Walter B. Miller of Harvard Law School's Center for Criminal Justice.

The reality of the above examples plainly demonstrates that America cannot control its alcohol and tobacco consumption, nor can it prevent its children from destroying themselves and the country's institutions. These are signs and symptoms of artificial brains in operation.

The inmates can see themselves very vividly when they hear the truth. Many inmates have shown that they have more insight upon receiving the teachings of Imam Muhammad (Warith Deen Muhammad), than the members of "free society". They see how their lives have been misdirected and they learn why. They question themselves to determine why they were unable to control themselves and, thus, resorted to criminal acts. They question why they never sought to dignify themselves, their communities and their country. They ultimately conclude that they were functioning with artificial brains.

In the field of corrections, study must extend into the communities from whence the inmates are produced. Correctional administrators must develop the courage and the sincerity to band together and attack the false mental images within the institutions as well as without. Corrections officials should not be satisfied to just treat inmates within the confines of prisons, and then allow them to be "thrown to the wolves" upon their release.

## WHAT IS PROPER HUMAN BEHAVIOR?

Proper human behavior can only be defined as that behavior which was demonstrated during the life of Prophet Muhammad, (Peace be upon him.) His behavior was governed and controlled by the Divine dictates of Almighty God, Allah. This is the only example of real human behavior that we have today that can accurately identify what is proper.

We cannot apply the usual definition of human behavior that is normally found in today's psychological and sociological studies. These studies define human behavior as **any and all singular or collective activity, or the lack of activity of an individual or group.** In short, according to some writers, " . . . . it is everything that a mortal does or does not do". (Source: Samuel Dixon and Robert C. Trojanowicz, **Criminal Justice and the Community,** p. 154, Prentice Hall, 1974, Englewood Cliffs, NJ). It is impossible to accept this endless range of activity as that of human behavior. We know that men and women in our present society (Western America), are capable of performing any and every kind of behavior imaginable.

The human being was designed by Almighty God, Allah and was made in the best of forms. His mission and purpose in life is to serve Allah alone in a conscious and willing manner. His duties are to be the khalifah (ruler) in the earth. He is to assume the responsibility for the welfare of everyone and everything in creation. The real human being's behavior is not to be altered in any way to please his wife, son, mother, father, daughter or anyone else unless it is in agreement with the laws of God.

Therefore, human behavior is not any and all singular or collective activity, or the lack of activity. The human being does not rob, cheat, steal, lie and murder. Nor does he destroy the good works of others. Proper human behavior excludes such activities as corporate monopoly in business to exploit the masses. It also excludes the establishment of governments that will deny its people the freedom to develop as human beings. Proper human behavior will support all virtues, deeds and traits such as honesty, prudence, patience, constancy, courage, faith and loyalty to Allah. Proper human behavior will support the needs of the widows and orphans, the sick and the indigent. It will bitterly oppose all corrupt forces that move to destroy human dignity.

We cannot afford to ignore our responsibility to cultivate proper human behavior ever again if we are to successfully attack the problems of corrections. Proper human behavior has to be cultivated in our society. The correctional officer must alter his weird concepts of human behavior. One cannot be a narrow-minded bigot and refer to bigotry as proper human behavior. Animals do not behave in this manner, and we have been given a far greater position and responsibility in this creation than animals. Human behavior should not be devoid of compassion and concern for other persons. Human behavior should express concern and respect for everything in creation. If you have a strong need to be respected, remember that the person you may seek this respect from should feel the same way. The correctional officer must absolutely know himself before he can begin to know anything about the inmates that are under his care and jurisdiction.

## IMAM WARITH DEEN MUHAMMAD'S
## EXAMPLE OF PROPER HUMAN BEHAVIOR

We mentioned earlier that Prophet Muhammad is the example or pattern that serves as the guide for proper human behavior. We have in our midst today another great man. Truly a blessing from Almighty God, Allah. This blessing, Imam Warith Deen Muhammad, is the living example and a demonstrator of how we should follow Prophet Muhammad (P.B.U.H.) I am a witness that Imam Muhammad's behavior is that of an excellent human being. It is through Imam Muhammad's proper human behavior that the total face, image, and direction of the Nation of Islam has been changed from one of separatism to that of universalism; from false religious worship to the pure worship of the One God whose proper name is Allah; and from anti-Americanism to healthy American patriotism.

Let us put this episode in its proper perspective so that you may better understand the significance of this great human being, Imam Warith Deen Muhammad. He was able to assume the leadership of The Nation of Islam in 1975 (a nation within a nation) which at that time was determined to physically separate itself from the Caucasion world of America. It was determined to make this separation because its members sincerely beileved that the Caucasian people were all a race of devils. Not only did the Nation of Islam believe that the Caucasian people of America were devils, it believed, with some doubt, that Black people were the "Black Gods" of the universe. This philosophy had been taught and internalized by the Nation of Islam for forty years under the leadership of the Honorable Elijah Muhammad.

Now, one should be able to see and appreciate the kind of behavior that has been and still is being exhibited by Imam Warith Deen Muhammad. Who else, other than a sincere human being, could have brought the Nation of Islam (now The American Muslim Mission) around to its present posture? Since proper behavior requires complete faith and trust in Allah (God), no other behavior could have manifested this grandiose change. Why do we say this? We say this because leadership develops in two ways: 1) leadership may emerge through the application of lies, corruption and deceit;

by manufacturing lies and building a world of false realities, strong demagogues will develop; 2) leadership will also emerge with the application of sincere faith, truth, justice and a reverence for Almighty God, Allah.

The initial foundation of the Nation of Islam was one of half truths, symbolic language, mysticism and one of the biggest lies ever told. (Since Allah (God) is bigger than all of creation, when a lie is told about Him, it is the biggest lie one can tell.) The Nation of Islam was based on the above concepts until 1975. It was at that time that the application of truth and sincere trust in Allah was introduced by Imam Warith Deen Muhammad. This book will not allow us to go into the details and history of the Nation of Islam, now known as the American Muslim Mission. But, one can now see how sincere proper human behavior will always dignify and raise the level of moral consciousness in the human being.

The correctional system will do well to study the teachings of the Imam (leader, one who is out front), Warith Deen Muhammad. He is not using guesswork. He is applying an exact science in the area of proper human behavior. Proper human behavior is not the distorted, corrupt activity that we now see the great majority of the people in our society engaged in. Drug addiction and alcoholism are distortions. Suicides and child molestations are distortions. These cannot be described as proper human behavior. These acts are performed by human beings, but the behavior is not proper for humans. It is sub-human.

# CHAPTER 8

# AL-ISLAM AS IT RELATES TO CORRECTIONS

## Part I

### The Principles and Pillars of Al-Islam

Al-Islam is that natural religion that teaches man balance. It structures his life and guides him throughout his existence. This religion is the same religion that was taught by all of the prophets from Adam to Muhammad (Peace be upon them.) This was the same religion that was taught by the Prophet Jesus.

The fundamental principles of faith in Al-Islam are as follows:

1. To believe in the One God (the Eternal, the Infinite, the Merciful and Compassionate).

2. To believe in all the Messengers of God without favoring one above the other. The one difference is their missions. Prophet Muhammad was the last Messenger and his message and mission were universal. His mission and aims are just as relevant today as they were 1,400 years ago.

3. To believe in the scriptures and revelations of God. These scriptures were used as guides which the Messengers used to show their people the correct path of God. In the Quran, a special reference is made to the books of Abraham, Moses, David and Jesus. But, prior to the revelation of the Quran to Muhammad, some of those books and revelations had been lost or corrupted, and others had been either forgotten, neglected or hidden. The only authentic and complete book of Allah in existence today is the Quran.( The Quran in the Muslim hands is complete.

4. To believe in God's angels (forces in creation). The muslim believes in the seen as well as the unseen. Knowledge and truth are not just confined to the sensory knowledge or sensory perception alone!

5. To believe in the last day (or judgment). This world will eventually come to an end. Every act or deed and thought have been accurately recorded and we must account for them on that final day. The Muslim believes in reward and punishment. He lives this present life in a manner that will allow him to receive his promised reward in Paradise. This life is just a journey which affords him an opportunity to earn his reward that is promised by Allah, who never fails in His promises. The Believer is punished for every evil deed he performs and every righteous deed is rewarded seven-fold.

These are the basic principles of the religion of Al-Islam. Realizing that these principles mean absolutely nothing unless they are practised, the Believer is ever God conscious. He keeps his mind on Allah and strives daily to live by these principles. What good are principles if they are not applied in one's everyday life? The Believer worships Allah (God) as if he can see Him, but he sees Him not. Every act performed by the Believer is done with the intentions of pleasing and serving Allah.

## THE FIVE PILLARS OF FAITH

The Muslim's religion, Al-Islam, is based on what we refer to as the five pillars of faith. While briefly discussing these pillars, let us imagine that we are constructing a tent. These pillars are as follows:

1. Belief in One God, who has no associates, no helpers, no fathers, no sons, no mothers. He is independent and is not in need of anything or anyone in this creation. He is the Creator, the Originator of all things;

2. Prayer: The Muslim is obligated to pray at least five times a day if he is physically able to do so. These prayers are offered: 1) Fajr—before sunrise, 2) Zuhr—immediately after the noon hour, 3) Asr—afternoon prayer, 4) Maghrib—after sunset and 5) Isha—night (evening) prayer. These prayers are performed to strengthen the Believer's faith in God. God does not need our prayers. We need His strength and protection;

3. Charity: (Zakat), The Muslim is obligated to be charitable. He may perform charity in many ways. Any good deed is an act of charity. Financially supporting the work of Al-Islam is an act of charity, helping an elderly person in need, etc.;

4. Fasting: The Muslim is obligated to fast during the month of Ramadan if he is able to do so. He must abstain from food and drink from sun up to sunset during this prescribed period. Fasting is done for Allah alone. During this period, we must be alert to always perform righteous deeds and study Al-Quran;

5. Pilgrimage or Hajj: Every Believer is obligated to travel to the Holy City of Mecca at least once during his lifetime, if he is financially and physically able to do so. He is required to perform the identical pilgrimage rites as they were performed by God's last Messenger, Prophet Muhammad (P.B.U.H.). The Hajj is considered to be the greatest regular conference of peace known in the history of mankind. Peace is its dominant theme.

The five pillars of faith form a tent with its center pole representing the belief in the oneness of God. The other pillars, 2) prayer, 3) zakat (charity), 4) fasting, and 5) Hajj extend the tent at four points from the center—North, South, East and West. This gives the Believer room for movement and growth within the structure of his religion. It affords him the opportunity for universal growth and development. This also points out to the Believer that along with his universal development, he has the potential for taking on universal responsibilities.

This brief description of the principles of Al-Islam and its pillars of faith is not nearly an adequate interpretation or explanation of this great religion. The reader must bear in mind that hundreds of thousands of books, articles and laws have grown out of this religion. We could not do justice to this religion of Al-Islam in these few pages.

These pillars and principles form the base from which the American Muslim Mission has successfully reformed many inmates. The American Muslim Mission is also striving to remake the environment from whence they came. These principles and pillars are being taught within the communities of all major cities of America and in other parts of the world.

The inmates' response to the religion of Al-Islam, being taught by Imam Warith Deen Muhammad, is positive beyond imagination. The Mujeddid (Imam Warith Deen Muhammad) has been blessed to be able to deliver this message to all men with such clear understanding that none can deny its truth. Man's human nature (his original nature) demands that he accepts the truth whether he likes it or not.

The inmate that accepts this truth, and does not fight it, becomes reformed almost overnight. I am not speaking from hearsay; I have witnessed this transformation myself. God put it in man's nature to accept the truth and respond to it when it comes. I have observed inmates evolve from one level of understanding to another, a level that promotes dignity and a mind to produce.

# Part II
## Al-Islam Addresses Problems in Corrections

The "new corrections" are following the premise that crime and delinquency are only symptoms of the failures and the disorganization of the society as well as of the individual offenders. According to correctional theorists, these failures deprive offenders of contact with the institutions that are basically responsible for assuring the development of law-abiding conduct, sound family life, good schools, employment, recreational opportunities and desirable companions to name only some of the more direct results.

According to the Task Force Report, "The task of corrections includes building or rebuilding solid ties between offender and community, integrating or reintegrating the offender into community life-restoring family ties, obtaining employment and education, and securing in the larger sense, a place for the offender in the routine functioning of society." (Source: Task Force Report: Corrections, p. 7.)

These objectives are noble and they are common sense goals. We have known the connection between social factors and crime in America since 1920 according to a series of studies carried out by Shaw and McKay at the University of Chicago. (Source: Clifford R. Shaw, Henry D. McKay, and others. "Delinquency Areas, A Study of the Distribution of School Truants, Juvenile Delinquents, and Adult Offenders in Chicago" (Chicago: University of Chicago Press, 1929)). These studies consistently showed high rates of delinquency in deteriorated areas within large cities, areas characterized by poverty and unemployment, residential mobility and broken homes, etc.

The University of Chicago, along with most large universities in America, has had its students do studies in similar academic areas. All of these studies have the same familiar ring. The criminal usually suffers from disrupted social conditions such as mental illness, suicide, alcoholism, narcotic addiction, incest, poor health, etc.

These studies simply reinforce the argument that the problems of correction within the Criminal Justice System have been manufactured. We must develop sound ways and means of reforming the inmate so that he will be capable of claiming his citizenship rights in America. We should also want him to be willing and able to assume the responsibilities associated with being a citizen in this society.

The individual offenders differ strikingly. Some seem to be irrevocably committed to being a criminal for the rest of their lives; they have spent more of their adult lives in prison than they have in society. Others simply do not subscribe to the values of this society or, they are aimless and noncommittal to any goals. Many are mentally disturbed and frustrated boys/girls and young men/women. Still others are alcoholics, narcotics addicts, victims of senility, or sex deviants.

With a problem of this magnitude, we should thank Almighty God, Allah, for blessing us with His last Messenger, Prophet Muhammad. (Source: Muhammad Husyn Haykal "The Life of Muhammad", North Atlantic Trust Publications, 1976—Library of Congress Catalog Card No. 76-4661, International Standard Book No. 0-89259-002-5). The University of Chicago refused to publish this book after previously agreeing to do so in 1968. Temple University also withdrew from its agreement to publish "The Life of Muhammad", by Haykal (We wonder why?). It is impossible for any man to consider himself a serious student of corrections, sociology, psychology, medicine, science, etc., unless he has studied something of the life of Prophet Muhammad and the religion of Al-Islam. Man's intellectual development is directly affected by his moral development. For example, one will not reach his intellectual potential without striving also to develop moral strength.

Prophet Muhammad (P.B.U.H.) established the religion of Al-Islam on the whole of the Arabian peninsula during his lifetime. Al-Islam along with its socially redeeming qualities, brought life to a people who were living in total social darkness. They were living in an age of ignorance. We must use the examples established by Prophet Muhammad in the area of corrections. Then we will be able to achieve success. Prophet Muhammad, through the blessings of Allah, established himself as the greatest social reformer in the history of this earth. The correctional system is in need of this same knowledge and leadership today.

Prophet Muhammad established a complete society based on the firm foundation of Al-Islam (truth and justice). The society was not shackled with the Western society's problem of the separation of Church and State. Prophet Muhammad's teachings of Al-Islam (complete and total submission to the will of Allah) produced a new world order and set the example for world society.

Al-Islam ushered in the Renaissance. It spurred the transition from the medieval to the modern times in Europe. The Renaissance man developed as a result of the teachings of Prophet Muhammad. The Europeans looked to the highly developed Eastern cultures for knowledge and inspiration. The culture of the Arabian peninsula, as well as African and other societies around the Mediterranean Sea, had been shaped by the teachings of Prophet Muhammad.

Prior to the mission of Prophet Muhammad, the social conditions in Arabia were practically devoid of concern for human dignity and individuals rights. The population cared little for reading or writing, and the women were considered merely articles of trade for marriage during this era (600 A.D.) For example, when a man died, his son inherited the wives together with the other property and chattel. A man's stepmother could become his legal wife. Wives could be bought and sold the same as donkeys, goats or any other commodity. A man could marry or keep as many women as he could afford and the women were rarely contented with one man. Lewdness and promiscuity were considered normal behavior.

The Arabs had no governmental system nor nationhood. Each

tribe conducted its own independent life under its chief. Many bloody rivalries would develop among them and there was always envy and jealousy between the tribes.

This brief description of conditions should give one some idea of the social conditions that Prophet Muhammad had to deal with. The people also were highly superstitious. They did a lot of reading of omens, drawing of lots, and they visited sorcerers. Many baby girls were either strangled to death or buried alive in the desert sands because the man felt it was a disgrace to father a girl.

Crime during this period was the norm. Killings would occur with the least bit of provocation. Many times a drunken brawl would explode into a blood feud between the tribes that would last for generations. Feuds would begin over such issues as racing of horses, cattle grazing, drawing of water, and these feuds would never end. Generation after generation fought and battled taking a life for a life and drawing blood for blood.

Prophet Muhammad's mission presented him to the Arab world during a period known as the Jahiliya (or the age of ignorance). Through the blessings of Allah, Prophet Muhammad united the Arabian peninsula and brought justice and mercy to that society. A total democracy was established based on the dignity of man. Governments were established along with necessary laws to allow local and national rule.

Crimes of robbery, murder, slavery, fornication and adultery were practically eliminated. Alcoholism and disrespect for women ceased to be a problem. These accomplishments are a matter of historical fact. The Europeans were brought out of their medieval condition (the dark ages) after the influence of Al-Islam began to impact their societies.

The Criminal Justice System must undergo a similar kind of reformation while using the above guidelines. Basic and sound principles under the guidance of God have been established and must be applied by the Criminal Justice System before it will reach its goal of prevention, protection and rehabilitation.

These are the weapons that we should be prepared to successfully bring to bare against the problems facing corrections today. We cannot approach the problem of corrections in America as some isolated problem. No! This is a universal problem. As the problem grows bigger in America, it will spread to the rest of the world.

When Prophet Muhammad (P.B.U.H.) was missioned by God (Allah), he was missioned as a universal prophet. Our leader today, Imam Warith Deen Muhammad, who is leading the Muslim community, is the universal Mujeddid of this day and time. Mujeddid means one who revives, brings back to the original, brings the freshness back that was there. He is the world renewer and the restorer of the religion of Al-Islam. It is because of Imam Warith Deen Muhammad's sincere faith and total dedication to serving Allah that he has been blessed with the knowledge to heal the social ills of America and of the world. The primary objective of the Mujeddid's mission is to restore the human being back to his original position of dignity and to show humanity that it must follow the guidance of God before it can solve its great social problems. He is the man who has inspired me to address the problems in corrections. He has addressed inmates and prison administrators of practically every State in America. The Mujeddid's keen perception of problems and their solutions are welcomed by every morally intelligent person who has heard him speak. One has but to examine the radical changes that the American Muslim Mission has undergone within the past five years, and he will agree that through the blessings of Allah, this man has performed more miracles than the Jesus of Nazareth.

What is his blueprint? Who outlined his plans and mapped his strategy? How did he gain the ability to inspire men like myself and others to go forth into this world and attack the evils of society relentlessly? What plan or strategy did he apply to change the total thinking of the American Muslim Mission (formerly the World Community of Al-Islam in the West)? He is applying Allah's plan. The Master Planner (Allah) has presented the world with the key to unlock the mysteries of life and death, and to restore man back to his proper place of dignity and self-respect. This should be the real aim and goal of America's correctional system.

To date, the religion of Al-Islam is being taught in practically every major correctional facility in America. [Those institutions that do not have formal or informal Islamic instructions are still strongly influenced by the teachings of this religion.] Every prison administrator that has supported the religion of Al-Islam with the same equity as he has supported other religions, can verify that this religion does bring about more peace, order, and stability among the inmate population.

For example, Dr. John Ramer, chief psychologist at Terre Haute, Indiana Penitentiary, stated that "the American Muslim Mission (formerly W.C.I.W.) has been helpful in transforming criminals into productive human beings". He also said," . . . it has helped give members a sense of identity with esteem. One is able to see himself as a part of a major religious group with meaningful existence and philosophy of life. It gives the members an opportunity to identify with something that would put a more constructive purpose in their lives than they had before". This statement appeared in an interview in the Bilalian News newspaper, January 4, 1980, p. 9. Another example of the redeeming powers of Al-Islam is that of a community of Muslims in the Maryland Correctional Training Center who are seeking to construct a Masjid (house of worship) within the confines of that prison.

This will not have been the first Masjid that has been built within a correctional institution, if Allah blesses these Muslims with success. Members of the Islamic community, in the Graterford Penitentiary in Pennsylvania, built a Masjid within the prison walls. The Federal prison system in the State of California has granted sole authority to representatives of the American Muslim Mission to regulate and oversee all Al-Islamic activities within that system. This came about through the direct efforts of Imam Warith Deen Muhammad.

A recent memorandum from California State Deputy Director, Walter E. Craven, addressed to Wardens and Superintendents in all Federal Correctional Institutions in the State of California stated:

"The recent video tape made of the Honorable Imam Warith Deen Muhammad, leader of the American Muslim Mission, along with George Warner, Assistant Deputy Director of institutions, and Superintendent McCarthy, presents an overview of the American Muslim Mission's rehabilitative efforts among the prison residents in correctional institutions."

" . . . . For the past several years, we have developed a cooperative and good working relationship with Imam Abdul K. Hasan, Western Regional Director of the American Muslim Mission."

The excerpts from this memorandum indicate that the positive teachings of Imam Warith Deen Muhammad has impacted one of the largest prison systems in America. This significant impact dictates that every effort should be made to make these teachings available within the prison system. In other words, the Federal government has stipulated that: **Our prison system should recognize the strong moral reform qualities of the religion of Al-Islam, as taught by Imam Warith Deen Muhammad, and we should take full advantage of it.**

In 1979, according to a survey taken by a Catholic leader, the Reverend Richard Houlahan (see Bilalian News newspaper, December 14, 1979, "Al-Islam's Progress in Federal Prisons"), there were approximately 25,000 federal prisoners, and about 1,500 (or 6 percent) identifying themselves as Muslims. The Reverend Houlahan also stated that almost every federal prison tried to accommodate the Muslim inmate's observance of Ramadan fast by making meals available either before sunrise or after sunset. His survey also indicated that 1,388 Muslim inmates took part in the Ramadan celebration, and 1,160 adhered to the fasting schedule throughout the 30 days. The Reverend Houlahan observed," . . . that's important because it demonstrates that the Islamics (Muslims) are well-motivated".

Fasting during the month of Ramadan is very significant in the life of a Muslim. Fasting is one of the five pillars of faith and a Believer fasts only to please Allah. He goes without food or drink from sunrise to sunset each day for thirty days. During this month, the Believer is to be constantly aware of Allah and His infinite blessings and mercy. He must abstain from listening to entertaining music, vulgarity, and arguments. He is to study the Quran and concern himself with the plight of those who are less fortunate than himself. He must abstain from sex during the daylight hours and must work hard to propagate (teach) the religion of Al-Islam.

One can readily see the valuable and redeeming powers of the fast during the month of Ramadan. A group of Muslims celebrating the month of Ramadan once a year within the institution has to exert a powerful influence of patience and perseverance among the other inmates. This group would be witnesses against institutions as well as other inmates who display arrogance, selfishness, greed and inhumanity toward each other. There are many valuable rewards that Allah blesses the Muslim with when he observes Ramadan. Allah also blesses those who aid others in their efforts to fast during this blessed time.

We can cite many examples that show how Al-Islam has made great strides towards helping the Criminal Justice System, corrections in particular. And, as the opportunities are broadened, Al-Islam will make even greater progress toward reforming not only the inmate, but the institutions and society as well.

In summary, we can say that we all agree that our objectives are the same. We want to reform the inmate but at the same time, we must reform and reshape his environment. This is necessary because the environment inside and outside of prison is immoral. For example, narotics, drugs and alcohol are readily available within the prisons and in society, along with other socially and morally destructive influences.

The next Chapter will deal with the application of Islamic principles inside the institution.

# CHAPTER 9
## AL-ISLAM SUPPORTS THE MISSION
## OF CORRECTIONS

The American Muslim Mission, under the leadership of Imam Warith Deen Muhammad, can best aid the field of corrections by keeping the correctional system focused on its goal or mission. The mission of corrections cannot be limited in scope. The discipline of corrections requires that its proponents be universal in their thinking; hence, its solutions must be universal.

The mission of corrections should be the restoration of its clients (inmates) back into the community while meeting the following goals and needs:

1. The inmate should be reformed (reshaped) and be able to constructively reenter his community.
2. He should be a responsible citizen.
3. The community should be reformed so that the ex-offender can live in an environment that is conducive to his future growth and development.
4. The environmental climate should be changed from that of a hostile, deceitful one, to that of a truly free and just one.
5. The ex-offender should represent strong moral and intellectual leadership in his community and should be willing and able to assist himself and others.
6. The ex-offender should have respect for everything in creation.
7. The ex-offender should begin to assume universal responsibilities.
8. The ex-offender should place all of his faith and confidence in God alone.

These goals are designed to complete the mission of corrections; therefore, none of them can be excluded. The aims and aspirations of corrections must, of necessity, be the same as those of all the Prophets. These aims and aspirations were all directed toward the establishment of a Universal Brotherhood of Man—One Humanity. The Criminal Justice System (law enforcement, judicial and corrections) must assume this posture. Reality of purpose demands that our mission ultimately offer a final solution to the problem.

It would be very naive to suggest that the pressing short term goals in these areas, specifically corrections, be ignored. Other needs that must be met are: 1) Immediate physical needs must be taken care of, 2) Of necessity, society must be protected, 3) The criminal must be punished or shown mercy, and 4) When the peace of the community is broken, it must be restored. These needs must be met if for no other reason than that our laws demand it. We know that our society must provide its citizens with basics, i.e., food, clothing, shelter, educational opportunities, equal employment and the pursuit of happiness (a safe environment).

In the process of dealing with these immediate needs, we cannot afford to lose sight of our original goal or mission. Corrections has been side tracked too long by only concentrating on immediate, if not emergency, needs. The correctional system has been operating with a plan of crisis management. The cycle of rushing about to supply the simple needs outlined above has to be broken. This cycle can only be broken with the clear, rational logic that comes from revelation (revealed knowledge from Allah (God)).

The field of corrections cannot avoid or ignore the great body of knowledge that the religion of Al-Islam offers toward solving its problems. When we talk about corrections, in essence, we are discussing the process of remaking a man. This is a very difficult task, to say the least. We, as mere mortals, do not possess the know-how. We know for certain that we first must make a determination of what kind of a man we want. I feel that we have adequately outlined the type of man that we should have, but we must agree on this. In order that we may come to an agreement on an issue as vital as this, we must consult the highest authority available to man.

The highest authority is Almighty God (Allah), and He has made The Holy Quran available to us through Prophet Muhammad. The Holy Quran is the perfect guide for all mankind, and it has no imperfections. This Book determines for the Muslim, and for all men, the kind of man Allah (God) intended to live in His creation. The correctional system cannot bypass this truth.

It is self-evident that no progress can be made in any phase of life unless there is a set objective. Corrections must have a set objective, a definite ideal, before it can be inspired to strong self-assertion.

The greatest inspiration to self-assertion is the overt aim to please God in one's endeavor, regardless of its nature. It is in the nature of man to please or satisfy God, and history has shown us that it is the God-inspired people and institutions that make the greatest progress.

The human being cannot come into unity with himself or his fellowman without the guidance of God. An effective correctional system cannot function without unity. The correctional staff and the inmates must be in unity. The support staff such as social workers, psychologists, psychiatrists, and teachers must be in unity. This bond of unity must also include the correctional administration as well as its Board of Directors.

The American Muslim Mission has recognized the necessity for man to have a guide by which to pattern his life. Through Imam Warith Deen Muhammad, this community was directed toward the example of Prophet Muhammad. We should understand why this man was selected as the perfect guide or exemplar for all men. Most of our scholars of scripture, the exegesists, and many religious leaders know that Prophet Muhammad is God's last and only **universal** prophet and servant. He was the only prophet that unified a whole society during his lifetime. The success that he achieved was amazing to both friend and foe alike. Prophet Muhammad was/ is the most successful and influential leader in the history of this earth. And, his success was based on the single and very simple principle of unity of purpose. The only purpose that can guarantee this degree of success is the single desire and aim to please God and God alone.

The religion of Al-Islam can support this mission of corrections by eliminating the fear, false pride and ignorance from the hearts and minds of those men and women who are presently working in corrections. Those individuals working at the administrative level are affected the most by the above mentioned elements. It takes a great deal of courage to stand up for truth, justice and righteousness in this world, especially in the field of corrections, because of the nature of the work itself. Sometimes you will be called upon to defend the rights of a man that, perhaps, is guilty of a very despicable crime. Many times political pressures are brought to bear against innovative prison administrators. Decision-making powers may be taken away from them, thereby relegating them to the role of a "figure head". This process may be referred to as "bureaucratic lockout". The individual affected may be either promoted in rank or demoted, but the effect is still the same.

The principle of Al-Islam cannot embrace a man that makes decisions based on fear of loss of prestige, employment, popularity, etc. The only fear Al-Islam supports is the fear of Allah. And, this is an intelligent fear. A Muslim fears to do anything that may displease Allah. Too often political decisions are made in corrections instead of practical, rational and logical decisions simply because of the above-mentioned fears. Some prison administrators fear their political sponsors more than anything in the world. Consequently, most substantive decisions that are made by them are made after they have consulted with and gotten the approval of their sponsors. These decisions include, hiring and dismissing personnel, prison programs, budget requirements, selection of private vendors, etc. This is common knowledge among correctional administrators and others, therefore, it does not require any documentation. There have been enough prison administration scandals in our local newspapers to confirm this charge.

Allah promises success to all men who fear Him and Him alone. Al-Islam makes it plain that Allah is well able to support those who do righteous deeds, and He promises success to the faithful. The correctional administrator should not seek to make a deity out of his political sponsor. This is a blatant form of idol worship. How can a prison administrator, in clear conscience, dictate policy affecting the lives of hundreds of inmates and staff personnel while he is bowing down to some corrupt politician, who in turn, is bowing to his constituency? This can produce enough hostility to destroy the decent spirit in everyone involved. Fear of doing what is fair and just is not tolerated in Al-Islam, hence, it cannot be tolerated in corrections.

False pride develops in man when he fails to give all credit for achievements to Allah. God deserves the praise for everything in creation because He made it. It belongs to Him, He maintains it, and He regulates it. Many of us come into positions of power, authority, and prestige because we acquire knowledge and experience in various fields of endeavor. Men begin to praise us or simply show us respect for the position we are blessed to hold. We, in turn, become "puffed up" with pride. Man begins to think that he rose to this position without any assistance. Hence, we have the type of correctional administrator that is egotistical, blind, deaf and dumb.

Correctional administrators must realize that God gives us intelligence and it is through Him that we learn. If we do not respect the Creator and cannot submit our intelligence and worldly accomplishments to Him, how can we possibly respect our fellow human beings and work comfortably with them? If we do not give all praises to God (i.e., glorify Him) in our successes, we will be blind, in that, we will not be able to see the true reality. We will lose our common senses and become morally and mentally blind, deaf and dumb. We have but to examine many decisions that have been made in the field of corrections and we will see that common sense has been lacking. For example, nationally, we have almost one million men locked up and about 80 percent of them are nonproductive. This is enough manpower to operate many multi-million dollar industries. Yet, the correctional system has failed to effectively utilize this manpower.

Ignorance is a major contributing factor to the present fragmented hit or miss correctional system. This book has pointed out many reality flaws that have brought us to this point. The religion of Al-

66

Islam enjoins us to seek knowledge. Prophet Muhammad encourages his followers to seek knowledge as far away as China. Education, in the field of corrections, is absolutely necessary. We cannot keep groping about in the dark. As we have pointed out earlier, revealed knowledge gives man logical explanations and answers to problems.

The correctional system does not have to stumble around like a drunk seeking a park bench to rest on temporarily, only to be chased away again by an alert park policeman. As we have pointed out over and over again, Prophet Muhammad, the man was the expert in the field of corrections. One Muslim writer recently wrote a short book entitled **Islam and Alcoholism.** The author, M.B. Badri, brilliantly demonstrated how Prophet Muhammad effectively eliminated the problem of alcoholism in the Muslim society. He applied revealed knowledge from Almighty God (Allah).

Our common sense should tell us that if God created us, He can also supply us with the answers to our problems. The correctional system has to have the courage to place the blame for most of its problems on the corrupt elements in our society that are perpetuating criminal activity. It must pull its head up out of the sand and face reality. The religion of Al-Islam supports this mission and guarantees an ultimate solution.

# CHAPTER 10
# THE CRIMINAL JUSTICE SYSTEM AND RELIGION

The Holy Quran speaks to the many social ills that are plaguing our society today. Even though The Book was revealed to Prophet Muhammad (P.B.U.H.) over 1,400 years ago, it is still just as relevant today and as important to human survival as it was then. The Quran contains all of the knowledge that society needs to solve the problems within the Criminal Justice System.

The Quran contains the revealed knowledge of the ages, knowledge from Allah, Himself. It is suggested that the history of the revelation of the Quran be studied by those who are skeptics. The Criminal Justice System, as we know it today, has evolved out of a Christian oriented society. Its laws, methods of enforcement, application of justice and interpretation of justice, as well as punishment, were developed along the path of the European Christian doctrine. Even though the Church and the State have claimed separation (that is, neither will attempt to infringe on the rights of the other), Judaic and Christian religious beliefs are very much a part of the Criminal Justice System in America.

The power of ecclesiastical tribunals to establish laws concerning marriage, testaments, the nature of sacrilege, the proper forms of sexual behavior and many other forms of human activities rose and fell over the centuries, as English Kings struggled with the authority of the Catholic Church. The Church continued in its struggle to regulate human behavior until the secular courts won the right to regulate these matters. But, history clearly shows that common laws became very much a part of the present day English law.

There is very little difference, if any, between English law in Europe and "English law" in America. After all, prior to the Declaration of Independence, America was simply an English Colony. Today, in America, a Judge must be sworn in by the Chief Justice prior to taking his seat on the bench. This swearing in process is done within the constructs of the Christian Church. This same process or procedure must be also acted out by the highest executive officeholder in the land, the President of the United States.

There are many other public service positions that require this same kind of swearing in or oath taking process prior to appointment. Even in private industry there are areas of employment and professions where individuals may be either encouraged or required to swear or pledge their allegiance by concluding with "in the name of Almighty God". Every witness that appears on the witness stand in court must agree that he will speak the truth to the best of his knowledge, "so help me God".

If one can agree that the Criminal Justice System evolved out of a Christian philosophy, our next step should be to determine whether or not this philosophy has been sound enough to support the system. It should be readily agreed that, thus far, the Criminal Justice System has failed completely in its mission to curtail crime.

Within the Bilalian (African-American) communities in America, crime has sky-rocketed, and there are no signs of abatement. "More Bilalians were killed by other Bilalians in the year 1977 than died in the entire nine-year Vietnam War. Most of the 5,734 Bilalians killed on the battlefields of Bilalian America in 1977 could have survived Vietnam since the Bilalians who died there (5,711) averaged only 634 per year". (Source: Ebony, More Black Killed on Street Than In Vietnam, Aug. 1979, Johnson Pub. Issue: Black on Black Crime) The victims and the offenders in the aforementioned statistics are members and a part of this strongly Christian oriented society; and as such, their ultimate behavior patterns and attitudes were strongly influenced and shaped by their Christian religious indoctrination.

The criminologists have refused to look at religion as being the underlying cause of human behavior. They are still operating under the illusion of secularism. This view of separating the "worldly" or physical life from the spiritual life will remain a burden and a yoke on the back and neck of the Criminal Justice System. A close examination of Christianity will show this same kind of fractionalism within its philosophy.

Hopefully, behavioral science will begin to move toward considering the presently underrated impact of religion in man's life. The human being is also an organic being. He consists of components that operate in unity and with balance. His physical development is directly related to his mental and moral (spiritual) development. The man's components must have continuity of purpose. Man's total development must evolve uninterrupted and his whole being must strive towards his life's goal or mission.

The human being's mission in life is ultimately determined by whatever he gives his life to. Accordingly, the world's leading authority on proper human behavior and religious interpretation, Imam Warith Deen Muhammad, says that the human being will give himself to practically any influence without the guidance of Almighty God (Allah).

Since man has the propensity to sacrifice himself for something, he will find himself on a suicidal mission of self-destruction without guidance. This profound factor in human nature must be considered by the Criminal Justice System if it is to be effective in altering human behavior.

Man will sacrifice his life to gain many things, such as power, fame and wealth. He must justify his reason for living and in doing so he is forever in search of his destiny. He seeks to completely satisfy every yearning that comes from his body, his mind and yes, his soul. The criminologist has to realize that without the proper channel that will enable him to fulfill his needs, his aims and desires, man will be destined to commit crimes as long as he is in existence. Man has been given limited free choice and free will.

The Quran was revealed to mankind in order that man may be rightly guided by Allah (God). Man, in his innocence, has always accepted guidance from that which he regarded as superior to him. As he develops his intellect, he becomes more selective in choosing whom he will or will not worship or give himself over to. If the man is sincere and is honestly seeking the truth, he will be guided to Al-Quran, and he ultimately will worship the one God whose proper name is Allah.

The goal of the Criminal Justice System and criminology should be to ultimately evolve into one institution that will be able to effectively alter the attitudes and behavior of its clients. These attitudes and behavior patterns must be altered to the extent that the offenders, upon their release, will be an asset to themselves, their families and society. These changes must be induced by human methods, and they (the methods) should be willingly accepted by the offenders.

The courts have attempted to protect the rights of the inmates as well as those of law abiding citizens, but have failed. The courts have failed for the reasons discussed previously. The courts, too, evolved out of a weak and corrupt concept of Christian religion. To date, there are no guidelines for determining the purpose of criminal sanctions. There are no guidelines to show justification for sentencing criminals. Hence, an offender in Chicago may be sentenced to 5 years for armed robbery and another offender in New York may receive a two-year sentence for the same offense.

Some law abiding citizens, who have appeared in court, will readily relate how unpleasant their experience was. Many times they are treated very shabbily by the courts, the States Attorney and the police officer. An objective observer would have difficulty determining whether the victim was the defendant or the complainant in some courts because of the indifference shown by some court officials. Some citizens in the Chicago area have expressed concern and apprehension about calling the police because of distrust due to past treatment received from members of the Police Department.

What can the Criminal Justice System or corrections, in particular,

70

do to overcome our problems? Since the legislators and judges have not agreed on the purposes of sentencing or punishment, what is to be expected of corrections? In theory, there are many specific motives for sentencing or punishment, but society has not agreed on any of them. These include:

1. **Prevention:** Preventing the criminal from committing further crimes by giving him unpleasant experiences he will not want to experience again.

2. **Restraint:** Protecting society from persons deemed dangerous because of past criminal behavior, by isolating those persons from society.

3. **Rehabilitation:** "Punishing" convicted criminals by giving him appropriate treatment in order to rehabilitate him and return him to society so reformed that he will not desire or need to commit further crime.

4. **Deterrence:** Deterring others from committing further crimes by causing the suffering of a criminal for the crime he has committed.

5. **Education:** Educating the public as to distinction between good conduct and bad conduct through the publicity which attends the trial, conviction, and punishment of criminals.

6. **Retribution:** Imposing punishment by society on criminals in order to obtain revenge on the theory that it is fitting and just that one who causes harm to others should, himself, suffer for it.

These penal objectives are firstly concerned with the individual offender (prevention, restraint, rehabilitation) and others focus upon the community (deterrence, education, retribution). These objectives have merit and should be generally agreed upon by society. But, society cannot arrive at a point of agreement without the guidance of Allah. Agreement can only come about through unity of purpose. The Quran and the Traditions (Sunnah) of Prophet Muhammad constantly remind mankind that the aim of Allah is the unity of humanity and humanity's sole purpose is to serve Him.

Hence, Allah provides the only determining force and truth that will bring man to agreement on crime and punishment, thereby giving mankind the guidelines he must have in order to establish a realistic Criminal Justice System.

The Quran speaks directly to crime and other offenses throughout its pages. And, Allah constantly reminds us, all of us, of what our responsibilities should be towards this end.

"O ye who believe
Fulfill (all) obligations.
Help ye one another in righteousness and piety,
... But help ye not one another in sin and rancour:

71

Fear God: for God is strict in punishment."
Holy Quran 5:1, 3
(Yusef Ali Translation)

Here, society is clearly given its duties. It is not to assist anyone who violates the laws of the land. Man cannot help a criminal by allowing him to go unchecked. Prophet Muhammad (P.B.U.H.), in his last sermon stated thusly:

"O people! Listen to my words and understand the same. Know that all Muslims are brothers unto one another. You are One Brotherhood. Nothing which belongs to another is lawful unto his brother unless freely given out of good will. Guard yourselves from committing injustice."

(Islam In Focus: Author, Hammadah Abdalate, p. 126, American Trust Publications, Indianapolis, Indiana).

The words of the Prophet are obligations to the Muslim. A Muslim is any man or substance that submits to the will of Allah. A study of this universe will quickly reveal that everything in creation submits his will and his total being to Allah whether he likes it or not. He must constantly sacrifice his life and his trusted possessions.

In concluding this Chapter, one can safely assume, without reservations, that the religion of Al-Islam can establish unity of purpose within the Criminal Justice System. The following penal objectives fit well within the structure and the guidelines of Al-Islam:

1. **Prevention:** It is the individual person and society's duty to prevent criminality, and if it is necessary that the preventive measure be unpleasant, so be it.

2. **Restraint:** The community must restrain individuals as an act of mercy and appropriately administer the death penalty.

3. **Rehabilitation:** The violator has no choice in the matter of altering his behavior. He must change or face rejection by the community. This is justice.

4. **Deterrence:** Allah has established examples among men as well as past societies in order that we may reflect (look back and see what has happened to those in the past who were disobedient to the laws of God). Allah speaks to mankind and reminds them of others who went astray, and He deters us accordingly:

"From those, too, who call
Themselves Christians,
We did take a Covenant,
But they forgot a good part
Of the Message that was
Sent them: so We estranged
Them, with enmity and hatred
Between the one and the other,
To the Day of Judgment.

And soon will God show
Them what it is
They have done."
(Holy Quran, Chapter 5, Verse 15)

5. **Education:** The great problem today is the general public has been miseducated and purposefully misguided so that crime will be increased. The Quran exhorts man to enlighten the people. Speak to man's intelligence instead of his emotions. The public must be educated with the Quran in order to clearly distinguish between good and bad conduct. Al-Islamic education is the key to success.

6. **Retribution:** This is clearly man's right. But, according to the Quran, he may waive his right to retribution if he so desires.

# CHAPTER 11
# MASS MEDIA AND ITS RESPONSIBILITY

Our local daily newspapers and other forms of mass media such as radio and television produce stories and news items that are primarily geared for the twelve-year-old mind. A close study of the materials produced on radio and television would indicate that they are designed only to hold the attention of a twelve year old. This is a sad indication of the intellectual state of our adult population. This media has been known to extoll the virtues of politicians who are able to answer a question without answering it, and praise the political figures that do and say what is politically expedient instead of what is right and just. The news media in America refer to honesty of figures in government as naivety. This is the promotion of crime at its worst. Former President James Carter was often referred to as a very simple, common man from the South, who was honest, but he was not viewed as politically wise.

The media uses various forms of propaganda to influence the behavior of most citizens in America. Many years ago, a study was done on the **Chicago Tribune** to examine the kind of "emotional stereotypes" it used. This paper was militantly opposed to President Roosevelt and his policies, and to the newly organized C.I.O. (S.S. Sargent, **Emotional Stereotypes in** The Chicago Tribune,). When referring to New Deal policies and practices and to organized labor in its news columns, the Tribune used such terms as "Czarism", "dictatorship", or "agitator", "communist" and the like; terms that it was possible to show, aroused negative emotional responses in people. Similarly, when referring to Republican policies and practices or to workers who refused to strike; the **Tribune** used such terms as "cooperation", "freedom", "recovery", the "right to work", etc.; all terms that evoked favorable emotional reactions.

In a more recent example, the **Chicago Tribune** began to attack the Mayor of Chicago (Mayor Jane Byrne) by using this same type of emotional appeal. The City of Chicago recently came under fire after three top police officers were demoted. These demotions, according to the officers involved, were prompted by organized criminal influence within the City administration. In writing stories related to this issue, the **Chicago Tribune** repeatedly used the term **"mob influence"** in describing and explaining the demotions and transfers of the police officials in question. The **Tribune** was not the only organ that applied this technique. Radio and television were, and still are, equally guilty of this kind of reporting.

Mass media uses various forms of emotionalism (propaganda)

to influence target groups. Communication specialists, according to some writers, find that the greatest success is with the more suggestible members of the population, such as younger people and those of the lower socioeconomic status. It has also been theorized that propaganda is most effective, by and large, when it is clear-cut, direct, and simple.

In the most progressive States, the average adult over thirty years of age has little more than a high school education or a minimum of one year of college training. This limited, non-quality education leaves the masses vulnerable to almost any subtle form of propaganda or subliminal suggestions. The masses have not been taught to think rationally, to heed or become alerted to information and the probable consequential outcome when this information is acted upon.

Therefore, when this "prepared" population hears, through the media, that the Palestinian people in the Middle East are terrorists and killers, it responds by looking at the total Arab people in a negative light. To date, when the Palestinian Liberation Organization (P.L.O.) launches a military operation against Israel, it is referred to as an act of "killing". But, when the country of Israel makes a military move against the Palestinians, it is referred to as a "bombing". The implication here is that dropping tons of high explosives in densely populated civilian communities does not really kill.

It is this kind of mind twisting that is greatly influencing the citizens in America. The behavior of most inmates was greatly altered in a negative way by mass media. Statistics have supported the fact that most inmates have never gone beyond high school in pursuit of education, and that high school education was inferior at best. (See **Profile of State Prison Inmates: Sociodemographic Findings from the 1974 Survey of Inmates of State Correctional Facilities.**) These statistics were compiled by the U. S. Department of Justice.

Since mass media is directed towards the masses (the poor), why does it constantly uphold wrongdoing in such sly and subtle ways? The mass media attempts to outwardly present a front of objective and honest reporting, but underneath, it is as vicious with its lies as Satan himself. It is this false reporting that the masses are fed. Let us not forget that 70 percent of the inmates in the correctional system have never finished high school. It is safe to say that they all were greatly influenced by the mass media.

At this point, it is not necessary to document hypocritical news reporting because it has grown to be almost common knowledge among the masses. But, recall the great prison riot at New York State Prison in Attica; the mass media reported that guards had been slain and mutilated by the inmates. The media also reported that some of the guards had been castrated. The public discovered later, after autopsies had been performed, that the guards were slain by the New York State Troopers, who recaptured the prison yard.

All forms of mass media must ultimately be held accountable for everything published or broadcast to the public. The media should not be allowed to publish or broadcast anything that is not true and not directed towards the betterment of humanity. Committees should be established by the Government that will demand that the media assume the commensurate responsibility along with its freedom to publish and broadcast healthy news to the public. Until such time as the media is held accountable and responsible, it will be one of America's biggest supporters of criminal activity.

## NEWS REPORTING ON CRIME

The news media habitually uses sensationalism to sell its newspapers and air time. Crime reporting is one of its foremost components. Street crime in America has grown so common that one wonders how the media still manages to use them to gain profits. The mass media will not be outdone, e.g., a street gang shooting is a very common occurrence in most of our major cities. Yet, the media begins its dramatics with a gang shooting by headlining the name of the gang, states the number of gang-related shootings, and possibly naming a few gang members.

This kind of reporting goes beyond the scope of informing the public about a criminal incident. It does several things: 1) It publicizes the gang, thereby lending legitimacy to the group. 2) It encourages youths that are not gang members to either join the gang, if you want attention and notoriety, or stay out of the gang. 3) It encourgaes individual gang members to try to commit even more sensational criminal acts for the sake of publicity and greater status within the gang. 4) It promotes emotionalism within the communities involved and generates an unnecessary urge for vengeance.

The mass media should publish criminal acts only with the intention of informing the public. There are so many crimes committed daily in large cities that if they were all put into newsprint and televised, we would not have time or space for anything else. Therefore, common sense should dictate that a standard method of crime reporting should be adhered to. Crimes may be reported simply by giving the number of offenses with reference to categories, i.e., robberies, burglaries, etc., the general location of the crimes and of available descriptions of wanted persons. There is no need to give the names of the victims or persons arrested. Names should

76

be mentioned in the media only after there has been a trial and conviction. The offender only then should be publicized. Television stations should not be allowed to publicize arrested suspects and victims unless publicizing is necessary to aid in the identification of persons or property.

The above suggestions, if applied, would prevent the media from being able to effectively use emotionalism in the sale of its news papers and air time. It would force the media to become more responsible in its reporting. These suggestions would eliminate a lot of crime, and the mass media would not lose one dime in income. There would be no financial loss because newspapers, magazines, radio and television have sold more than enough ads to publish their works before they are printed. The public still wants to be informed and does not mind paying for it.

The real culprit behind the mass media is that devil-minded corrupt Jewish interest, that satanic mentality that comes to feed the masses emotionalism and subtle lies. This is a serious problem, and we must address it if we are going to be effective in the correctional process. Crime has to be fought at all levels of society and on all fronts.

Mass media has constantly attacked and ridiculed prominent leaders including the President of the United States. Editorial cartoons and slanderous jokes about the country's leaders are subtly designed to undermine the public's respect for leadership. Once it has been suggested to the mind of the public that the President of the United States is an idiot, by way of a cartoon or a cruel joke, it is very difficult for the President to come before the public and be accepted totally as a serious and responsible leader. Leadership must be respected in order that institutions can survive; institutions cannot survive without leadership.

The importance of leadership within the individual must be emphasized at this point. If the inmate is not taught respect for leadership firstly within self, then within society, his life is always going to be filled with unnecessary problems that he could have avoided had he been taught and educated to respect leadership. Leadership begins within the individual at birth. Every member of the individual's body responds to the leadership of his intelligence. The focus of mass media is to influence man in such a way that he will ignore or totally disrespect all forms of leadership.

# CHAPTER 12

## "MASS MEDIA AND RELIGIOUS SYMBOLISM AS CRIMINAL INFLUENCES"

There have been many brave attempts made by serious scholars to demonstrate how mass communications is used to help influence and shape our society in America. These efforts have either been ignored through ignorance or by design. The public has been programmed to disbelieve the allegations that the media is being used in such a diabolic manner. Not until Imam Warith Deen Muhammad began teaching has the general public shown any real interests in mind manipulation by mass media.

Modern scholars such as Wilson Bryan Key, Harold Innis, Theodore Thieneman, Alvin Toffler and others have ventured into the area of symbolic language. They have attempted to arouse the public by intense research in their efforts to prove that the media applies symbolic language and images to control the habits of man in our society and, hence, his destiny. None of these men, thus far, have been able to grasp the full depth of understanding, the real application, nor the real impact of these seductive, symbolic methods of mass communications.

When Imam Warith Deen Muhammad began to teach on this subject, we began to realize that the aforementioned men were thinking at a very elementary level. Mr. Muhammad has taken us back into history and has shown us clearly how truth has been consistently hidden or locked in symbolism. The objective then is the same objective today—to control man by directing his life through false images and symbols. For example, the Holy Bible is loaded with symbolic and seductive language. In America, just a few years ago, the Bilalian minister was not allowed to teach the accepted religion of Christianity unless he had the picture of a Caucasian man portrayed as Jesus, the Son of God, displayed before the people.

The teachings of all the Prophets, who presented the people with revealed logical knowledge was intentionally corrupted. This corrupted knowledge was widely disseminated. The Bible is the greatest puzzle ever presented to the world through the common mass media. We know that when the truth is twisted and presented to innocent and gullible minds, a crime is committed, e.g., the media advertises cigarettes in such a manner that they appear attractive to the potential buyer, but he is uncaring as to the full physically damaging effects of smoking.

The Caucasian image of Jesus Christ, as our Savior, was presented to the world as a divine person with powers equal to God. Imam Warith Deen Muhammad shocked the world when he addressed this false symbolic image with these questions:

"Were Christ Jesus to be put in Black skin, wooly hair, blunt Bilalian or Afro-American features, widely published and revered and given the same place in worship occupied by the White traditional image, what would be the effect on the world after several generations of identifying the Black racial images as the (Supernatural) God in the flesh?

When a little Bilalian (Black or African-American) child and a little 'White' child sit side-by-side during Church service before the Christ in the flesh, or on the cross, or images that are otherwise displayed, what is the psychological affect on these two (2) children?"

Imam Muhammad follows these questions with an appeal to all persons concerned about the welfare of the human being. "Let the new world return to the pure divine commandment. Make no images. Support our plea that Americans abandon racial effects in the worship of God. Thank you."

He asked another question pertaining to this subject. "What would happen if 'White' people were to sit in Churches for 300 years with the image of a Black man on the cross? What would this do to their minds?" It is this kind of false seductive teaching that has been disseminated among the world masses. This type of seduction had a far more damaging effect than Mr. Wilson Bryan Key could have imagined when he addressed the problem.

He was primarily concerned with conducting a study in an attempt to prove that:

1) "there exists in the human brain and nervous system something (a mechanism of uncertain description) responsible for such labels as the unconscious or the subconscious. That this machinery exists can be empirically demonstrated, beyond any doubt, to be a vital aspect of human behavior in all its manifestations."

This writer demonstrated in his work, **Subliminal Seduction,** that mass media was conducting an assault against the public and it had the specific ability to manage, control and manipulate human behavior. This is done in the interests of a multi-billion dollar national economy. His work entailed using over one thousand test subjects to prove that pornographic pictures and sexual language, hidden within the pictures of ads such as Gibley's London Dry Gin caused a very strong mental reaction in some of the subjects. (Source: Wilson Bryan Key, **Subliminal Seduction.** Prentice Hall, Inc., Englewood Cliffs, New Jersey, 1973).

Mr. Key was also deeply concerned about the health dangers

that may result in mind manipulation. He discovered some of the after effects upon interviewing his test subjects. He observed that:

"Subliminal persuuasion can be even more dangerous to mental health. In the service of commercial profit, highly skilled technicians are probing into and manipulating the most intimate, subtle and complicated mechanism of the human nervous system—a mechanism still virtually a mystery to science."

We are delighted that Mr. Key has expressed this concern, and we encourage him to study what Imam Warith Deen Muhammad is teaching. Imam Muhammad has been given the knowledge to expose Satan's tricks to the world. We know that the media manipulators are mere imps who are doing Satan's bidding. Yes, we agree that mass communications media is being used to exploit the public financially, but the greater evil is its application toward reinforcing the mentality of ignorance that the world is already under. Prior to the advent of mass media, false knowledge, symbolic language and spiritually intoxicating concepts had already been fed to the people of the world.

This kind of knowledge (false religious doctrine) appealed to the emotions and the passions of the masses. Now, we are seeing the results. The element of love in man's nature has been turned to lust (e.g., a mother continues to protect her son even though she realizes he is committing criminal acts in the community). She knowingly accuses other people in the community, such as the teacher, policeman, and his accusers of "picking on him." This mother is not showing love for her son through this kind of behavior. She is really lusting for her child's affection, in that, she does not want to lose favor in his eyesight. Here the mother demonstrates an obsessive desire to protect her son from punishment even though he is wrong. This abnormal behavior will cause the son to grow strong in his weakness.

This mother, in all probability, if she is a Christian, will also claim great love for Jesus. But, in reality, it will be the same form of lust that she exhibits for her son. The Bible language also suggests that Jesus's body should be eaten and his blood be drunk during a ceremony referred to as the Eucharist (Communion). Here, this so-called love for Jesus is easily transferred to lust for his physical body, and promotes a sense of cannabalism.

Let us listen to the kind of religious language that has been used down through the ages and we should be able to see, with ease, that the appeal is not directed toward our intellect. Take for example, the Orthodox Jewish concept of **"God's chosen people"**. This language plainly states that the Jew is God's chosen people. We are also taught under this doctrine that you can only be a Jew by birthright; and, there are only two kinds of people on earth, those are Jews and Gentiles. Many times in the Bible, the Gentile people are referred to as "my little children" or "children of God".

If the above language is accepted, anyone that is not Jewish cannot get close to God unless he gets close to the Jew; nor will he ever be allowed to get as close because he was born a Gentile. Therefore, he has to accept the Jew as his leader (father) or mediator between him and God. Here we see man is called upon to place himself in a subserviant position to another man in order to get closer to his Creator, God. In essence, if man accepts this concept, he makes a God out of another man and hence, the seduction process is complete.

The acceptance of this concept was the beginning of racism. We have shown in previous paragraphs how racism was applied in religion. The corrupt Jewish religion began to separate the world's people based on skin color and nationalistic boundaries. This kind of language has led to the destruction of many societies because of its power to fragment the thinking of man and destroy the unifying concepts that bind men together. That is, the belief in one God, and hence, one creation and one humanity.

If man's thinking had not been tampered with or influenced by false knowledge, he would have known that God has no chosen people, associates or partners. Our intelligence would tell us that the person with the most righteous heart is the closer one to God. The man who is morally upright, bound by faith, truth and reverence to God is closer. This is common sense.

Another example of religious language that appeals to your emotions is that "Jesus died for your sins". Now the world is presented this pitiful looking image of a Caucasian on the cross. He is almost nude, he is very frail looking, his hair is long and stringy, and he has cruel wounds in his hands, feet and on his body, and he looks almost feminine. Why was this done? Whose idea was it? What purpose was it intended to serve? After this image was presented to the world, the world was informed that this man came back to life and is now equal to God.

Upon examining the language, we will find that the masses are being told many things. We are being told that we were sinful and that someone died for us. We are also told that we do not have to be responsible for our behavior because we are born sinful, therefore, we cannot control our own behavior. A Caucasian died for us so the people of color should be grateful and serve him because he is the Son of God. He is also God the Father, God the Son and God the Holy Ghost. We should always worship man especially if he is

Caucasion. Therefore, we should worship ourselves. We are told that God allowed this to happen to himself, which suggests that we enjoy pain especially when it is self-inflicted. We are told that we should suffer peacefully. God did it and if it is good enough for Him, it is good enough for us.

This image and language as you can see is loaded with seductive influences that have sunk deep into the subconscious mind of the people. The mass media of today is merely used to trigger the "artificial" brains that were implanted into the heads of the world masses centuries ago, and the people of color in particular. This image has already aroused the public sexually in its subconscious mind. Homosexuality has been suggested along with many weird forms of behavior that should be alien to the human being.

We all should be able to agree at this point that, if the same mind that produced this image of a Caucasian on the cross is presently in control of the mass media, it is exerting the same influence over the people today as it did thousands of years ago. Therefore, we must conclude that the mass media, as it is presently used, is a major unseen criminal in our society.

The correctional theorist is obligated by reality to consider the above analysis. He should feel bound by respect for the truth to seek answers to the questions that were posed in the previous paragraphs. Case studies of the individual inmates would reveal that much of their negative behavior was influenced in the above-described manner. I have, personally, talked with many criminal offenders and sought logical answers from them explaining why they committed a particular offense. I received very few, if any, logical responses. In reflecting back, I do not recall ever being given a logical reason for committing a crime except through fear of personal safety or ignorance. These offenders, in committing these acts, were responding to subconscious programming.

Criminal behavior is controlled, to a large extent, by mass communications media. This can readily be proven if we take the following steps. We can simply use mass media to present a message of concern to the people from Imam Warith Deen Muhammad. Crime would be drastically reduced within a four-month period or less. It is within man's original nature to respond to the truth when it is presented to him with understanding. We realize that the private controlling interests of the mass media are not going to accept this challenge because it is not in their best interest. Their interest, as we have previously indicated, is assisting in controlling the people by influencing, then dominating their minds.

The leaders in the field of corrections should collectively demand that this be done. The field of corrections is large and has the potential to generate the kind of pressure that is ultimately going to be needed to force the mass media to correct itself. Why should we allow the media to promote criminal behavior? The State correctional facilities are controlled by the people of the State through elected officials. The Governor of the State, an elected official, normally appoints the Director of the State Correctional System.

An examination of most penal institutions will reveal that pornographic magazines, books and papers are readily available to each inmate. These are materials that can only create problems or aggravate existing problems within the institution. The prison administrators have the authority to screen the kind of materials that are allowed in the cells of inmates. The kind of television and radio programs that place an abnormal amount of emphasis on sexual behavior and acts of violence can readily be controlled. Why allow mass media to promote abnormal behavior within our prisons when we do not have to?

There is a great problem of homosexuality within the walls of our institutions. The problem of rape among inmates is a national disgrace. Many television programs are beginning to boldly exploit and display homosexual behavior. Other criminal acts are encouraged in the same manner. It has to be suggested at this point that a committee be established within each institution to screen all mass media program (television and radio), magazines, periodicals and books that primarily speak to purient interests and other criminal propensities.

Inmates should never be allowed to have free access to any and all programs and materials presented through the mass media. The controllers of the media are morally bankrupt and place no limitations on what will go over the TV screens, radios or into printed matter. Mass media checks its behavior only when pressure is brought to bear. We often hear news reporters openly inquire about an interviewee's sex life or ask other bold personal questions that are designed to destroy or disrupt the peace of any reasonable human being.

Mass communications media is controlled and managed by very shrewd and intelligent people. This block of people universally concerns itself with manipulating the opinion of the world masses. It can readily be said that they are in the business of disseminating information or educating the public. It has been determined that crimes are committed by individuals who are the victims of misinformation or lack of information.

Mass communications media has had the opportunity to educate

83

the masses in a rational and logical way, but it has failed to do so. Instead of appealing to the intelligence of its readers, listeners and viewers, mass media in the main has appealed to man's emotions as well as his baser nature. The average citizen, capable of only performing elementary feats of reading, writing and arithmetic, can conduct a simple survey himself that will condemn our mass media.

For example, if one views television for a twenty-four hour period, they would find that very little time is given toward educating the public in a sound moral way. Eighty percent of the viewers and readers' time is consumed by sports, gossip, meaningless talk shows, commercials and stories that actually are insults to human intelligence. The viewer conducting this survey will find his human nature being assaulted by many types of weird pictures and false concepts. He is given demonstrations on how to commit adultery, robbery, incest and treason by simply watching television or listening to his radio for 24 hours.

This kind of information is being constantly fed into the conscious and subconscious minds of every man, woman and child who is exposed to radio and television in America. Media manipulators are aware of what they are doing. It is no accident that religion is no longer taken seriously by the media. The manipulators have successfully turned our society away from the worship of God. The dignity of man can only be protected through its reverence for God. Intelligent fear of Allah is the only solution to crime in America and the world. Mass media is aware of this, hence, it constantly strives to keep its viewers and listeners focused on every issue except serious worship of God.

Daily newspapers are sold every morning in each major city in America, 365 days per year. The average American adult seek his daily newspaper in an almost religious way. If sports scores are not made available through the newspapers immediately, roughly half of our population would be in a state of mental depression and confusion, due to shock. Radio and television stations have viewers and listeners in all major cities for 24 consecutive hours, without let up. Prime time television shows boast proudly that they have millions of citizens in America viewing their national networks.

This great flood of communications has to assume its burden of responsibility for educating the public about crime. The public can very easily be fed a regular diet of strong moral and intellectual teachings without any problem. Educational programs that encourage moral development will strengthen the social fabric of our society, thereby discouraging criminal acts. The criminal develops not because he lacks intelligence. Major criminals in our society are found to be very high on the intellectual scale, but very low on the moral scale.

Therefore, mass media is obligated to establish consistent programs with strong moral leadership directing its every move. Imam Warith Deen Muhammad is the only man who is presently capable of directing this task. He has demonstrated his ability through the evolution of the American Muslim Mission and the **A.M. Journal.** The media, when properly used in the promotion of human dignity at every level, can eliminate crime practically overnight.

Behaviorial scientists have demonstrated that if they have control over B, they can alter B's behavior. Is it not safe to say that the media has control over a miseducated public? That is, a public that has not been taught to think and move with rational sense and clear logic? It is ludicrous to argue that our public is rational in its thought processes when it is suffering from all kinds of perverted and aberrated ideas and concepts about life.

For example, a large majority of Americans are still superstitious. Many are visiting palm readers, fortune tellers and determining their moves by horoscopes. The problems of alcoholism, child abuse, insanity and homosexuality are just a few signs that clearly show that the American public does not collectively think and move rationally. If it did, these problems would have been eliminated or reduced to such a significant degree that they would hardly be a threat to our country. Many so-called primitive societies do not have these problems.

Hopefully, we have now arrived at the conclusion that mass media has a large miseducated public at its disposal, a public that it has irresponsibly manipulated on its "merry-go-rounds", ferris wheels and loop-de-loops of emotionalism and high sensation. Is it not time for the public to come out of its lethargic state? Crime is tolerated by the public because the public is kept in a constant state of abnormal mental drowsiness by the mass media. The mass media in America can be justifiably and criminally charged with reckless conduct, in that, it has in some instances committed acts or omitted some acts, that induced criminal behavior on the part of its readers, listeners and viewers.

Mass media's argument against these charges is that "you can't prove it". Of course, the public cannot prove or convince the media that it is criminally liable because the media managers live in an unreal world of fantasy. Whenever one assumes that the public is too ignorant to be trusted with truth, knowledge and understanding, he has erroneously placed himself in a divine-like position. He is now determining what the public should or should not be taught.

All human beings have intelligence. Therefore, when the media assumes that it cannot speak to the public's intelligence, it is living in an unreal world.

If the public ever places the media on trial for the above-named offences of criminal negligence or reckless conduct, the media most certainly would be found guilty. Crime is on the rise. It will not cease until the media is called to task. The Department of Corrections will always be attempting an impossible mission so long as it allows mass media to impact it negatively.

# CHAPTER 13
# THE OFFENDER'S RESPONSIBILITIES

This society cannot allow a convicted offender to abrogate his/her citizenship responsibilities. The correctional system must be charged with the duty of seeing that the offender's behavior is governed by the same dictates and responsibilities as any other citizen in society. Why should the convicted offender be allowed to drop all of his duties and responsibilities to his family, his community and his country? This is not justice. The victim still has citizenship obligations. He/she is expected to be productive and remain an asset to the community. The victim is required to work on his/her job, support his/her family and pay taxes to support the local and national institutions of the country.

The American Muslim Mission (A.M.M.) demands of its members equal responsibility in the maintenance of its community. Prophet Muhammad (P.B.U.H.) in one of his Hadiths said that the man that labors hard to supply his own needs and that of others has far greater worth than the man that prays all of the time. What right does this society have to allow convicted men to live in idleness, or engage in non-productive activity? The correctional system in America has to be given the responsibility of gaining the best use of the inmate's time while he/she is a part of this system. Almighty God, Allah, is a working God. He neither sleeps nor eats, and He is constantly looking after man's best interest. Are men any better than He, the Creator, Sustainer and Maintainer of all things?

Positive productivity is demanded of all human beings by God Almighty. Therefore, when society denies the correctional system the authority and the support to seek positive productivity from the offenders, it defies logic and reasoning. One develops his/her mental, physical and moral strength by constant use. These qualities must be utilized constantly in order that they may increase in strength. In other words, man has to develop his mental muscle by using it. He must subsequently balance the development of his mental muscle by developing his moral and spiritual muscles.

This is the only way that man can evolve into the human being that Allah intends for him to be. The inmate must not be allowed to "stagnate" while he/she is incarcerated or involved in a community based program, that is, parole, probation, work release, etc. If the offender is only required to accept his sentence, and idle away his time in any of the above-mentioned situations without being responsibly accountable to society, we will all suffer a great loss. Because if this situation exists, the offender will be ultimately released, and this extended period of idleness will have made him weaker and less able to aid the community than he was prior to his conviction.

Man develops in three stages: 1) He first develops as a physical creature. He is motivated by physical needs or drives, i.e., food, clothing, shelter and other comforts. During his struggle to acquire these needs, man is driven to develop his intellect. 2) The intellect must develop as man observes the need to overcome his physical shortcomings. Not only is man's intellect sharpened in order to compensate for his physical limitations, it is sharpened because of his innate curiosity, his quest for answers to the many questions that Allah's (God's) creation causes man to wonder about. 3) The third stage of man's development is his spiritual and moral growth.

Man's spiritual and moral development must, out of necessity, be allowed to grow naturally. This will determine his relationship to Allah, and hence, his relationship to his fellowman. If this three-stage development does not take place naturally and with good balance, man will develop as a cripple. He may be either too intellectual in his thinking or too spiritual. Or, he may develop morally strong and neglect his intellectual growth. The correctional system must be given the responsibility, under law, to see that all offenders are encouraged and aided in these life developing stages.

The formula for implementing this program has already been worked out, tested and effectively applied. We indicated earlier that it was implemented by Prophet Muhammad (P.B.U.H.), 1,400 years ago, and it is being successfully applied today in the American Muslim Mission by our leader and teacher, Imam Warith Deen Muhammad. A man who has never really understood how he is supposed to evolve as a human being can gradually be brought into this knowledge. Once the offender can really see and understand how his total life is dependent upon his developing in the above prescribed manner, he will gladly accept duties and responsibilties within the institutions. Not only will he accept these duties, he will dignify them and himself.

The correctional system has to stop thinking with the Jahcubite mentally, i.e., that the common people cannot be trusted with knowledge. The offenders in our institutions will respond to revealed knowledge, that is, knowledge that has been revealed to God's prophets down through the ages. The inmates are no different from many other members in our present society, nor are they any different from the people of Arabia during the time of Prophet Muhammad. There are many members in our society that have committed greater crimes than some of our present inmates. They have simply managed to evade our criminal justice system, or we are too burdened to deal with them.

It is being suggested that offenders be given commensurate responsibilities within the correctional system, as are all citizens in this society. The mechanics of making the offenders assume their in-house responsibilities can be very easily worked out. The leader of the American Muslim Mission is always available to assist America in a universal effort such as the one we have proposed. In the interest of logic and reasoning, of justice and mercy, and of reverence for God, the offender must be willingly led into the path of human dignity while they are within our correctional system.

## THE SPIRITUAL NEEDS OF THE OFFENDER

What dignifies the human being? This is a strong thought provoking question that the correctional system must address. It must also ask another question such as, what debases the human being? These questions were presented to a group of student Imams by our Leader, Imam Warith Deen Muhammad. We all made our contributions towards supplying the answers to these questions. But, of course, we all were delighted to hear our leader's response to his own questions. These are not his exact words, but the meaning can be understood. He said that man is dignified when he develops the ability to recognize that Almighty God, Allah, is a greater power than he is. Man is further dignified when he shows a willingness to submit, totally and completely, to the will of Allah. Man will reach his ultimate peak of dignity when he is able to surrender everything that draws him away from God.

In answering the second question, "What debases man?", Imam Muhammad responded by saying that, when man rejects the truth, the power and existence of God, he debases himself. Man, in his arrogance, debases himself when he rejects the Holy Quran, the pure Book, the "light". Man is made in the best mold. He is made to logically respond to revealed knowledge. When he rejects it, he is debased. In order to exist as a strong worthwhile human being, man must have strong faith and belief in God. This is the only way that he will remain focused on his universal destiny.

The correctional system cannot continue to function without considering the spiritual needs as well as the other needs of its clients. It (the correctional system) must be discriminating enough to examine the source of these needs. We firmly believe that the development of gangs within the institutions is indicative of the lack of sound spiritual guidance and revealed knowledge (knowledge and guidance from Prophet Muhammad P.B.U.H.). The inmate has to be guided away from having to exist in an animal-like "free for all environment". The human being was not intended to exist in this manner.

Animals are "clocked" (programmed) by nature to live in an environment of the survival of the fittest. Man's original nature demands that he support the weak, the sick and the needy. It is against his nature to take advantage of the weak. Therefore, the correctional system must emphasize that it is the duty and responsibility of all offenders to protect all men from all evils whenever they are able to do so. No offender should be allowed to abrogate his responsibility to protect a fellow inmate or custodian from unjustified physical attacks.

The leisure time of the inmates should be used for constructive re-creation and not recreation. He should re-create himself first through the guidance of God and, secondly, he should begin to improve the prison environment. He should clean up the mental and moral atmosphere by setting a righteous example for everyone.

# CHAPTER 14
## THE PRISON SOCIETY

Our juvenile and adult correctional institutions are beset with many varied and serious problems. Some of these problems are lack of security and safety of the inmates and correctional officials, and also mis-management, economics, and political interference. It is these problems that create the setting of a society that automatically forms within the walls of our institutions.

Specifically, the society within the adult institutions is composed of the same character of individuals that one will find in any major city in America. The prison society has, indeed, a higher concentration of convicted criminals. But, a metropolitan city such as Chicago, New York, or Los Angeles has, perhaps, more criminals roaming freely than we would find in all of our State penitentiaries.

This analogy was made simply to focus attention on the prison society and not just view it as a criminal society. It is a fact that the members of the prison society are criminals, but their society is not necessarily criminal.

There is a formal organizational structure within the institution, but it does not fulfill the total needs of the inmate. Subsequently, an informal structure develops, and it is through this mechanism that the inmate attempts to fulfill his total needs. Hence, we have the development of a prison society. It may be referred to as a subculture by sociologists or it may be called an informal organization. But, this society functions, in that, it meets some of the needs and goals of the inmates.

The prison administration has not been mentioned until now in order to emphasize this point: **even though the prison administration forms the foundation for the formal organizational structure by virtue of its authority, the prison society could very well exist without it.** This, of course, is provided the prison society is supplied its basic needs. The basic needs of the individual inmate are also the basic needs of the inmate society. By definition, a society is an organized group of persons associated together for religious, benevolent, cultural, scientific, political, patriotic, or other purposes. It also means human beings collectively associated or viewed as members of a community. A society normally seeks to furnish protection, continuity, security and identity.

Upon accepting that a prison society does indeed exist, it is a national responsibility of the country to give this society and others like it—proper guidance. The problems that exist within our institutions most certainly exist in the civilian population. These problems vary only in degrees of significance. The steady flow of complaints of criminal assaults, inadequate health care, lack of educational opportunities and unemployment come from both prison and civilian societies. Other complaints of homosexuality, drug abuse, lack of police protection and official corruption sound familiar to everyone. The prison society is also tested with these same problems.

The prison society, not unlike others, is also pluralistic in its composition since America is a pluralistic society. Hence, its penal populations will most likely reflect this ethnic, religious, and cultural mix. Within the aforementioned areas of social differences, there are further breakdowns in group compositions that must be considered. For example, the Bilalian prison population represents 47 percent of the total in the State penitentiaries. Within each prison that has a significant population of this ethnic group, one will find close knit sub-groups such as members identified with street gangs, religious organizations, associations, Black nationalist groups, clubs, etc. This same social condition exists among Caucasian inmates who have, in some instances, identifiable Klux Klux Klan and Nazi organizations as well as religious and social organizations.

The Criminal Justice System has successfully funneled the social mix of humanity into its correctional component without any workable plan for reconciling their varied ethnic and social differences. The Spanish-speaking prison population has not been mentioned, but it has increased considerably, and it is also impacting the social order of most of our state institutions. In some states, such as New Mexico, Texas and Arizona, there are sizeable groups of Mexican-Americans within their prison populations. In 1974, the Hispanics represented 7 percent of the total state prison population numbering approximately 12,359 inmates. These statistics are available through the U.S. Department of Justice, **Profile of State Prison Inmates.**

This society will not be able to function with a positive attitude unless it has at least one common identifiable goal. This goal must be one that each subculture and the administration can identify with. Studies have indicated that institutions that did not have treatment goals and programs will experience a higher degree of hostility between inmates and the administration. Prior to initiating any treatment program, the general attitude of the population must be responsible in a positive way.

Institutions that concentrate their efforts on strictly custodial concerns will also encourage the development of dictatorial leadership among the various inmate groups. This response develops because the inmates are pressed to seek relief in the only way that appears logical to them. This strict custodial position will also pave the way for the hardened criminal to build his own artificial empire. Custodial personnel that is morally weak assist in this process. They will occasionally succumb to bribes because of fear or greed. This kind of behavior encourages more solidarity among the inmate sub-cultures and increased hostility and disrespect for the administration.

The most fundamental and essential common denominator that can be shared by all inmates is this: They are all human beings created by God. They all have the same human nature regardless of their ethnicity or social background. This principle of the oneness of humanity through the grace and mercy of our Creator is the only foundation that will support prison programs or custody, of course; but, custody alone without programs has its inherent problems. These problems, as we have indicated, can be more abrasive than the problems of treatment institutions. The principle of the oneness of humanity under God will eventually eliminate the stress suffered by both the inmates and prison administrators.

The common identifiable goal of a single humanity working together to bring about better working and living conditions will appeal to every inmate and prison staff member. To say that the appeal will not be successful is to deny the existence of human intelligence. The human being will respond to force. He can be threatened and forced to do many things. But, it is not normal behavior on the part of the human being to respond to force or threat of force simply because he meets superior physical strength. Therefore, the appeal to his intelligence is an absolute necessity.

The human response to force or threat of force is one of defense. One is obligated to defend himself against a threat or physical force. He defends himself in prison by immediately obeying, or, he obeys grudgingly. In a prison setting, the inmate is constantly made aware of his helplessness. The primary reminder of the inmate's helplessness is his lack of freedom. He is physically a prisoner, a captive of the state. He is legally constrained and confined in a prison by the people of the State.

The attitude of the prison society will change in a positive way when a constant appeal is made to its intelligence. The attitude can be shaped or oriented so that the inmate will obey orders and abide by prison rules and regulations without the threat of force. We have previously discussed methods that have been used to influence behavior in our society. These same methods can be applied within the prison society. But, it is important that the influence factor be one that is designed to uplift and dignify the prisoner as well as the administration.

The prison society is not a separate independent organ. It is a part of the United States of America, and as such is managed by the people. Therefore, prison society, by law, under the Declaration of Independence and the Constitution of the United States of America, must, of necessity, come under the same laws by which all other societies in America are governed. These same principles of the above-mentioned documents can be applied within the prisons. Granted, the prison setting is not the ideal place to apply these principles, but the Declaration, "We hold these truths to be self-evident, that all men are created equal, that they are endowed by their Creator with certain inalienable rights", is a strong statement that cannot be ignored.

Some prominent criminologists such as Norval Morris and Gordon Hawkins support the contention that the Criminal Justice cannot be moralistic. It is this attitude being reflected by accepted "Authority" that has perpetuated problems within the correctional system. These men have stated that, "We must strip off the moralistic excrescences on our Criminal Justice System so that it may concentrate on the essentials." They go on to say that, "the primary function of the criminal law is to protect our persons and our property."

The moral base of our Criminal Justice System must be as strong as we can possibly make it. The prison society looks closely at the administration for guidelines that are morally right and just. Granted, the inmate society has been convicted of some of the most heinous crimes imaginable. It has not shown compassion nor has it been just toward its victims (society). But, the human being will always seek justice and moral strength from those who are in a position to regulate his life.

The prison society and its individual members are more demanding of justice and fair treatment within the institution than its members demanded of the civilian society when they were free. For example, many inmates will demand the right to have access to the showers at least once a day. But, when they are free, some of them would consider it insulting if it was suggested that they take a shower every day. Prior to their arrest and conviction, some inmates would have literally fought to the death to avoid taking a shower or a bath each day. When they are free, they never demanded access to soap and water. Why? Because they were selfishly going about their business in a free world and were primarily attempting to satisfy their wants in a "free for all" society.

This "law of the jungle" mentality is very much curtailed to a significant degree once a man is incarcerated. Hence, he concerns himself with basic human rights. The very rights he readily deprived his victims of are now being demanded by the inmate. The prison

94

society realizes that basic human rights are fundamental if prison life is to be made tolerable. It should also be noted that regardless of how much of a "brute" an inmate may be, he still seeks the virtue of honesty, compassion, mercy and unselfishness in others. In other words, if anyone is going to have anything to do with regulating one's life, the first thing that one wants to know is, does this individual (the regulator) have a heart.

We may conclude this Chapter with the understanding that each prison society regardless of its ethnic makeup, collectively, has the same needs as any other society. Its individual members seek basic human rights, hence, it is conclusive that the total body must have the same goal. The Constitution of the United States must continue to be used as the basic guideline in our pursuit of a just prison society.

The application of the Constitution (which is a Quranic document) will support the prison administration equally as well as it will support the inmate. But, the relationship between the administration and the prison society must be clearly understood and maintained. The administration must, of necessity, represent the leadership of the prison society. This prison leadership is obligated to demand the best from its followers, but at the same time it must be tolerant of each other's shortcomings.

# CONCLUSION

The process of corrections within the constructs of the Criminal Justice System will not take place until the individual's mind seeks to correct itself. Attitudinal changes will not occur until the mind seeks reality. The one reality that man must accept before he can be corrected is that he is a part of this creation and that there is only one Creator. The inmate must come to the realization that every individual must have an intelligent fear and respect for God.

When the inmate arrives at a point during his incarceration that he has reverence for God and an intelligent fear of God, then he is well on the road to recovery, to being corrected. The Criminal Justice System cannot exclude Allah (God) from influencing its organizational structure. Every system is going to be influenced by something. Would you rather our Criminal Justice System be influenced by Al-Islam or by the State?

Remember, historically, our system has been influenced by the religion of Christianity. This corrupt form of religion was not able to impact the system effectively and now religion is regarded as a joke in most of our institutions. The religion of Al-Islam is presently bringing about gradual changes in American society that are healthy. These changes are also gradually taking place within the Criminal Justice System.

We are presently at a cross-road in our Criminal Justice System that will determine its success or failure. The public cannot tolerate the present high cost of crime. Maintaining prisoners within our correctional institutions at such astronomical costs has become very burdensome. Our country can very easily be convinced that there is no longer a need to support prisons. "Why not just slay all criminals who are presently incarcerated?" This is a question that is often asked by citizens in America. "Why should inmates enjoy air-conditioned quarters when most citizens in America cannot enjoy the same privilege?"

We are suggesting here that, if there is no concerted action to bring the influence of religion, primarily Al-Islam, into the correctional system, it is doomed to failure. This same statement can be made of the Criminal Justice System and America. I have argued rather strongly and effectively that the religion of Al-Islam has the answers to the problems facing the Criminal Justice System.

It is your responsibility as citizens in America and as universal human beings to assist in encouraging our society to do what is just and fair in the eyes of Allah to make our Criminal Justice System a reality. Correct knowledge and guidance is useless if it is not applied or accepted. I hope, at this point, that a portion of my duty to Allah has been fulfilled in writing this book. A Believer has the responsibility of delivering the message. But, we are not charged with overseeing man's affairs after the message has been delivered. All guidance comes from Allah.

All praises are to Allah Alone
Lord and Cherisher of the Worlds.

# BIBLIOGRAPHY

**As the Light Shineth From the East,** Imam Warith Deen Muhammad, 1980, W. D. Muhammad Publishing Co., Chicago, IL.

**Capital Punishment,** 1978, U.S. Department of Justice: National Criminal Justice Information and Statistics Service, 1979.

**Holy Quran:** Text Translation and Commentary, Abdullah Yusuf Ali, 1946, McGregor & Werner, Inc., Washington, D.C.

**The Challenge of Crime in a Free Society,** U.S. Government Prining Office, Washington, D.C , 1967.

**Corrections and Prisoners Rights,** Sheldon Krantz, 1976, West Publishing Company.

**Correctional Institutions,** Robert M. Carter, Daniel Glasier, Leslie T. Wilkins, 1972, J.B. Lippincott Company.

**Criminal Justice System and the Community,** Robert C. Trojanowicz, Samuel L. Dixon, 1974, Prentice-Hall, Inc.

**Profile of State Prison Inmates:** Sociodemographic Findings from the 1974 Survey of Inmates of State Correctional Facilities. U.S. Department of Justice: National Prison Statistics Special Report SD-NPS-SR-4, August, 1979, U.S. Department of Justice: Law Enforcement Assistance Administration: National Criminal Justice Information and Statistics Service.

**The Social Reality of Crime,** Richard Quinney, 1970, Little, Brown & Co., Inc.

**Subliminal Seduction,** Wilson Bryan Key, 1973, Prentice-Hall.

**Expenditure and Employment,** Data for the Criminal Justice System, 1977, U.S. Department of Justice, Law Enforcement Assistance Administration, National Criminal Justice Information and Statistics Service, Vol. SD-EE, No. 12 and State and Local Government Special Studies, No. 89, Issued May, 1979.

**Task Force Report: Corrections,** The President's Commission on Law Enforcement and Administration of Justice.

**Crime in the United States,** 1978, F.B.I. Uniform Crime Reports Release Date, Wednesday, P.M., October 24, 1979, U..S Department of Justice.